AN AUTOBIOGRAPHY

AN
AUTOBIOGRAPHY

By

R. G. COLLINGWOOD

with a new introduction by
Stephen Toulmin

CLARENDON PRESS · OXFORD

Oxford University Press, Walton Street, Oxford OX2 6DP

London Glasgow New York Toronto
Delhi Bombay Calcutta Madras Karachi
Kuala Lumpur Singapore Hong Kong Tokyo
Nairobi Dar es Salaam Cape Town
Melbourne Auckland

and associates in
Beirut Berlin Ibadan Mexico City Nicosia

Published in the United States by
Oxford University Press, New York

ISBN 0 19 824694 3

Copyright Oxford University Press 1939
Introduction ©Stephen Toulmin 1978
First published 1939
First issued as an Oxford University Press paperback 1970
Reprinted with introduction 1978, 1982

Printed in Hong Kong

CONTENTS

CONTENTS

PREFACE

THE autobiography of a man whose business is thinking should be the story of his thought. I have written this book to tell what I think worth telling about the story of mine.

Because an autobiography has no right to exist unless it is *un livre de bonne foi*, I have written candidly, at times disapprovingly, about men whom I admire and love. If any of these should resent what I have written, I wish him to know that my rule in writing books is never to name a man except *honoris causa*, and that naming any one personally known to me is my way of thanking him for what I owe to his friendship, or his teaching, or his example, or all three.

R. G. C.

CONISTON,
2 *October* 1938

INTRODUCTION
Stephen Toulmin

WHAT is the secret of an autobiography that lasts? Benvenuto Cellini sweeps us along with a certain shameless bravura. We cannot help wondering what kind of scrape his self-aggrandizement will get him into next. Gwen Raverat's *Period Piece* enchants us, by capturing a time or a place with the dust still on its wings. (She is clearly a great charmer, too.) Winston Churchill commands attention. He has lived through eventful times and played a prominent part in those events, so we are obliged to overlook his tendency to lecture us. By contrast, Thoreau is endearing, not least because he plays our own unspoken Arcadian dreams back to us. (Walden Pond was no wilderness: he could drop in on Emerson or the Alcotts any afternoon he pleased.) Every autobiography, it seems, is as individual as the life and personality that it represents.

Certainly, the individuality of R. G. Collingwood's autobiography helps explain why it still reads so well now, forty years after it was composed. It is written as well as all of Collingwood's books: that is to say, written with care and directness, rather than with any conscious elegance or attempt to please. It takes us through an intriguing stretch of social and intellectual history, ending on the brink of the Second World War. But the Oxford of John Cook Wilson and H. A. Prichard, H. H. Joachim and H. W. B. Joseph, was

by no means the central focus of original philosophical debate during the years between the World Wars,
and besides, Collingwood gives us a picture of that
world from a very personal angle. Again, the author
comes through to us as a straightforwardly truthful
man, rather than as a clubbable personality. Nothing
can wholly disguise the uncompromising character of
the 'dominie' whose scholarly detachment we see
crumbling under the impact of the Nazi era.

If we come back to the *Autobiography* with pleasure
now, it is chiefly because in it Collingwood succeeds
in doing what he set out to do—namely, to show us
the progress of one honest man's mind through a
difficult time. We are neither especially captivated
by his personal idiosyncrasies, nor particularly
fascinated by the situation in which his career placed
him. What holds our attention is the manner in
which, as his life goes along, the effects of situation and personality catalyse and enhance one
another.

Among Oxford philosophers of the 1920s and 30s,
R. G. Collingwood had the reputation of being a lone
wolf. He could never bring himself to go along with
any general party or opinion. Rather, he was one of
those English nonconformists who are fated to end up
by creating a party of one member. Reading about his
early life, we see that the basis for this intellectual
self-reliance was laid in childhood. He had the free
run of a happy, busy, cultivated and artistic home, in
which he escaped the domination of school, church,

or common opinion. Music, and reading from a well stocked library, then won a place in his mind that boarding school could not efface later on. So, he went up to Oxford with the habit of forming his own ideas in his own way and his own time, and it was not to be expected that he would subsequently become any more malleable or partisan.

Collingwood's eventual blend of history and philosophy was something in which few of his philosophical colleagues at the time shared much interest. Neither the New Realists among whom he grew up nor the Analytical Philosophers who began to displace them in the Oxford of the mid-1930s were at all historically minded. Yet it was scarcely possible for them to dismiss him—as they did G. R. Mure and the other idealists at Merton College—as a mere follower of F. H. Bradley. It was easier for them to shunt him aside and disregard him, with the suggestion that he was really an ancient historian, and had wandered into philosophy under a misapprehension. So, intellectually speaking, Collingwood had come by 1938 to feel very much alone; and the irritation and scorn with which he himself reacted to the philosophical situation at Oxford just before the Second World War led him to say some harsh things about his colleagues, which have been slow to be forgiven.

In part, the trouble was that Collingwood needed a bigger pond than the Oxford of his time provided. By the early 1920s, he tells us, 'I was now cut off not only from the "realist" school to which most of my colleagues belonged, but from every other school in England, I might almost say in the world.' Unfortunately, he did not really know what the rest of that world contained. He acknowledged some agreement with Benedetto Croce, whose admiration for Vico he shared. Had he lived in a more cosmopolitan time—for instance, in the years following the Second World War, when visiting appointments would have taken him regularly to the United States—he might have felt less isolated, and have ended by writing less stridently.[1] As things turned out, it was only after the *Autobiography* was in print—as an outcome of a Mediterranean voyage in the summer of 1939, with a group of Rhodes Scholars and others, chronicled in *The First Mate's Log*—that we see Collingwood at last reaching out towards his natural allies, in America and elsewhere. But by then it was too late. He came ashore at Naples on 16 August 1939, two and a half weeks before the outbreak of the Second World

[1] In his powerful and important book, *An Essay on Metaphysics* (1939), for instance, Collingwood launched into an intemperate attack on psychology, whose claims to standing as a science he dismissed as trumpery. What passed itself off as the science of the human mind should be recognized, he declared, for what it alone had the intellectual power to be: namely, the history of ideas. (If we are to study *how* people think, we must look and see *in what terms* they think. Ergo: 'cognitive psychology' is the same thing as 'conceptual history'.) However, if his experience had been wider and his reading of psychology more charitable, he might have discovered that much the same arguments as his own had long since been current within the field of psychology itself: at least, ever since the turn of the century, when Wilhelm Wundt was writing about *Volkspsychologie*, or the relativity of 'cognitive functions' to their cultural and historical contexts.

War, and this was still going on when he died, in 1943.

Nowadays, Collingwood's philosophical arguments speak to us more directly and forcefully than they did to his Oxford contemporaries. The 'realist' positions put forward by John Cook Wilson at Oxford, Ernst Mach in Vienna, and G. E. Moore and Bertrand Russell at Cambridge—like their counterparts in the United States—turned the philosophical clock back before Kant, and revived the earlier traditions of British empiricism.[1] Collingwood was one of the first philosophers in England to see that this could not be done. The realist doctrine, as he tells us here (p. 26), 'was rendered plausible by choosing as examples of knowledge statements like "this is a red rose", "my hand is resting on the table", where familiarity with the mental operations involved has bred not so much contempt as oblivion'. Yet ignoring those mental operations did not abolish them. As Kant had insisted, 'Percepts without concepts are blind.' The rational mind is actively involved in even the simplest of perceptions, so that what we 'make of' our sensory inputs depends on what we unthinkingly bring with us to the act of perceiving by way of prior mental apparatus—concepts, categories, forms of intuition, or whatever.

[1] For Moore and Russell's 'sense data', and Mach's *Empfindungen*, read Hume's term, 'impressions'. To the end of his long life, Russell used to speak of Kant's influence on philosophy as a disaster!

This criticism of 'realism' and the 'sense datum theory' has by now been accepted by most of Collingwood's successors at Oxford.[1] But Collingwood took a further step also, whose importance has been generally acknowledged only recently. It is not just that we arrive at knowledge only by bringing some prior mental apparatus to bear on our experience. A question must also be raised about the nature and credentials of that apparatus: 'Does it, as Kant assumed, take a single, universal form for people in all cultures and epochs—even, for all "rational thinkers", as such? Or are the basic forms that give structure to our knowledge subject to variation from culture to culture, and from epoch to epoch, as Hegel and Marx argued?'

Immediately after completing the *Autobiography*, Collingwood turned to write his *Metaphysics*, in which he presented a case for the latter, historicist position. All human thought (he there concluded) is confined within the particular constellation of 'absolute presuppositions' accepted in the individual thinker's culture and epoch. And, when we trace out the manner in which such constellations displace one another in course of time, we can do so only as historians of ideas. There is no unchanging, Olympian viewpoint available to us, from which we can judge

[1] Witness J. L. Austin's *Sense and Sensibilia* and P. F. Strawson's *The Bounds of Sense*, two of the most influential philosophical books to have come from Oxford in the last 25 years. John Austin's epigram, 'Sense data are dumb'—i.e. sensory inputs do not, by themselves, *tell* us anything—is a clear echo of Kant's assertion about the 'blindness' of mere percepts.

the comparative merits of different absolute presuppositions by timeless philosophical standards.

In the last fifteen years, a cruder version of Collingwood's position has obtained a certain currency and familiarity, through the popularization of T. S. Kuhn's theory of 'paradigms'. But a similar, subtler historical critique underlies a good deal of contemporary philosophical discussion. Many philosophers of science today, for instance, are preoccupied with the historical and philosophical problems associated with conceptual change. Meanwhile, among moral and social philosophers, a book such as Alasdair MacIntyre's *Short History of Ethics* reads like an extended commentary on the arguments presented in pp. 62–4 of Collingwood's *Autobiography*.

Even so, the justice of Collingwood's analysis is not yet universally recognized: notably, at Oxford itself. Peter Strawson, for instance, places great emphasis on the fundamental position for metaphysics of something that he calls 'our everyday conceptual framework'. It is not hard to imagine what Collingwood's reaction to this position would have been.

Just *whose* 'everyday conceptual framework' are we to take seriously? Consider a community of animists living in a nomadic forest culture. Is it entirely clear that they must necessarily share, e.g., Euclidean ideas about spatial relations, or our own industrial, citified notions of causality? People who grow up in circular huts without access to machine-made products (it turns out) even experience different optical illusions from those of us who live in square houses, surrounded by rectangular and linear artefacts. So, how can we take it for granted, like Kant and Strawson, that 'rational experience' is going to be structured alike in all cultures and epochs?

Far from Collingwood being an ancient historian who had blundered into philosophy, therefore, his admirable historical work on Roman Britain was—if anything—a by-product of his philosophical interests. Judging from the *Autobiography* alone, we might even form the impression that his professional concern with historical research was a footnote or afterthought, designed simply to illustrate his philosophical positions. This would be a misreading. Early on, Collingwood rejected the idea that philosophy was a specialized discipline, to be engaged in only by single-minded scholars who never let their formal arguments be corrupted by extraneous matters. On the contrary, working as an active research historian was one way in which he himself hoped to keep his philosophy honest.[1] In his archaeological and historical inquiries, he had of course to satisfy his own historiographical conscience. (If some histori-

[1] For similar reasons, many philosophers of science today find it necessary to keep up with new results in the natural sciences. This, too, appears to them a better way of keeping their philosophy of science honest than confining themselves to rewriting science in 'the typographical jargon of *Principia Mathematica*'— Collingwood's phrase: see p. 35, note 1.

cal colleagues complained that his digs tended, as a result, to 'turn up' just those things his prior questions had predisposed him to discover, that showed only that academic historians can be as committed to specialization as academic philosophers.) But Collingwood never tipped the scale in favour of philosophy and against history. For he always required his philosophical arguments—about the method of 'question and answer', and the rest—to prove their worth also in practical terms, in the course of actual historical investigations.

It is worth recalling that, when Collingwood first encountered ancient history, the subject was in some disarray. The work of Schliemann at Troy, and of Arthur Evans at Knossos, had made the recovery of Antiquity a matter of popular interest, a craze, even 'big business'. In the excitement of discovery, serious intellectual questions were thrown into shade by the beauty of Minoan frescos and the glitter of Agamemnon's Mask. Digs were conducted in a manner that appears to us, in retrospect, undiscriminating and needlessly destructive. Crates of material unearthed from the ancient sites of the Aegean and Levant were shipped off to the museums of western Europe, where some of them remained unopened for many years. At times, it was hard to tell whether the most fashionable archaeologists were moved by the enthusiasm of children or by the cupidity of grave-robbers.

Against this background, Collingwood's historiographical arguments represent a necessary return to the concerns of science and scholarship. The primary business of archeologists and historians is not to dig up art objects for display in museums—gapers at King Tut, please note!—so much as to formulate and answer significant questions about past modes of human life and thought.[1] Thus, for Collingwood, it was not just his work in history and archaeology that helped to keep his work in philosophy on track. His philosophical concern with 'method' also helped, for him, to keep archaeology and history honest.

To sum up: we have here the self-told life-story of an English academic, seen from Oxford just before the Second World War. It is the story of an English academic who exemplified many of the best features of the species. Unswayed by fashions, intellectually self-reliant, he was no less capable of loving or admiring colleagues and teachers with whom he publicly disagreed. (They were not always as charitable in return!) The severity and stiffness of the academic are clear enough in his story. But so, too, is his refusal to use the academic life as a refuge from the larger world of politics and international affairs.

Back in 1939, some of his responses to events in that larger world appeared terribly harsh—as, for instance, when he writes at the very end of the present autobiography of 'the minute philosophers of my youth' as 'the propagandists of a coming Fascism'.

[1] Chapters X and XI of the *Autobiography* are a better statement of Collingwood's historical principles, in this respect, than the longer and more complex essays in *The Idea of History*, collected together by Collingwood's friend, T. M. Knox, and published after his death, in 1946.

In a Britain that was finally pulling itself together and girding for the struggle with Hitler, Collingwood's bitterness was hard for his Oxford colleagues to stomach. Subsequent historians who have studied the political role of All Souls College in the 1930s, as an intellectual base for the 'appeasers', may see his comments in a different light. No doubt, he was going too far when he tarred John Cook Wilson with a brush that was more deserved by such men as Geoffrey Dawson. (Maybe, as he says, 'Fascism means the end of clear thinking'; but not all muddled thinking was on that account Fascist propaganda.) All in all, however, the record of Oxford academics during the early and middle 1930s, in standing up against the enemies of intellectual liberty and representative government at home and abroad, was not so very much better than the record of their counterparts at Heidelberg and Göttingen.

So, hindsight allows us to redeem, in Collingwood's favour, the claim that was most hotly challenged at Oxford when the *Autobiography* first appeared: namely, its claim to honesty. We have no right to assume that the painful words with which the book closes were any more of a pleasure for Collingwood to write than they were for his colleagues to read. Rather, we should accept the book for what its author declared it to be—*un livre de bonne foi*.

CHICAGO,   STEPHEN TOULMIN
May 1978

I

BENT OF A TWIG

UNTIL I was thirteen years old I lived at home and was taught by my father. Lessons occupied only two or three hours each morning; otherwise he left me to my own devices, sometimes helping me with what I chose to do, more often leaving me to work it out for myself.

It was his doing that I began Latin at four and Greek at six; but my own that I began, about the same time, to read everything I could find about the natural sciences, especially geology, astronomy, and physics; to recognize rocks, to know the stars, and to understand the working of pumps and locks and other mechanical appliances up and down the house. It was my father who gave me lessons in ancient and modern history, illustrated with relief maps in papier-mâché made by boiling down newspapers in a saucepan; but my first lesson in what I now regard as my own subject, the history of thought, was the discovery, in a friend's house a few miles away, of a battered seventeenth-century book, wanting cover and title-page, and full of strange doctrines about meteorology and geology and planetary motions. It must have been a compendium of Descartes' *Principia*, to judge by what I recall of its statements about vortices; I was about nine when I found it, and already knew enough about the corresponding modern theories to appreciate the contrast which it offered. It let me into the secret which modern books had been keeping from me, that the natural sciences have a history of their own, and that the doctrines they teach on any given subject, at any given time, have been reached not by some discoverer penetrating to the truth after ages of error, but by the gradual modification of doctrines previously held; and will at some future date, unless thinking stops, be themselves no less modified. I will not say that all this became clear to me at that childish age; but at least I became aware from reading this old book that science is less like a hoard of truths, ascertained piecemeal, than an organism which in the course of its history undergoes more or less continuous alteration in every part.

During the same years I was constantly watching the work of my father and mother, and the other professional painters who frequented their house, and constantly trying to imitate them; so that I learned to think of a picture not as a finished product exposed for the admiration of virtuosi, but as the visible record, lying about the house, of an attempt to solve a definite problem in painting, so far as the attempt has gone. I learned what some critics and aestheticians never know to the end of their lives, that no 'work of art' is ever finished, so that in that sense of the phrase there is no such thing as a 'work of art' at all. Work ceases upon the picture or manuscript, not because it is finished, but because sending-in day is at hand, or because the printer is clamorous for copy, or because 'I am sick of working at this thing' or 'I can't see what more I can do to it'. In myself I found less aptitude

for painting than for literature; from an early age I
wrote incessantly, in verse and prose, lyrics and fragments of epics, stories of adventure and romance, descriptions of imaginary countries and bogus scientific
and archaeological treatises. A prolific habit in regard
to such things was encouraged, demanded indeed,
by the family custom of producing in manuscript a
monthly magazine, circulated among a few friends
and relations. My mother was a good pianist, and
used to play for an hour every day before breakfast;
sometimes in the evening as well, to a surreptitious
audience of children sitting on the stairs in the dark;
in this way I got to know all Beethoven's sonatas and
most of Chopin, for these were her favourite com-
posers, though not mine. But I have never been able
to master the piano for myself.

My father had plenty of books, and allowed me to
read in them as I pleased. Among others, he had kept
the books of classical scholarship, ancient history, and
philosophy which he had used at Oxford. As a rule I
left these alone; but one day when I was eight years
old curiosity moved me to take down a little black
book lettered on its spine 'Kant's Theory of Ethics'.
It was Abbott's translation of the *Grundlegung zur
Metaphysik der Sitten*; and as I began reading it, my
small form wedged between the bookcase and the
table, I was attacked by a strange succession of emotions. First came an intense excitement. I felt that
things of the highest importance were being said
about matters of the utmost urgency: things which
at all costs I must understand. Then, with a wave

of indignation, came the discovery that I could not understand them. Disgraceful to confess, here was a book whose words were English and whose sentences were grammatical, but whose meaning baffled me. Then, third and last, came the strangest emotion of all. I felt that the contents of this book, although I could not understand it, were somehow my business: a matter personal to myself, or rather to some future self of my own. It was not like the common boyish intention to 'be an engine-driver when I grow up', for there was no desire in it; I did not, in any natural sense of the word, 'want' to master the Kantian ethics when I should be old enough; but I felt as if a veil had been lifted and my destiny revealed.

There came upon me by degrees, after this, a sense of being burdened with a task whose nature I could not define except by saying, 'I must think.' What I was to think about I did not know; and when, obeying this command, I fell silent and absent-minded in company, or sought solitude in order to think without interruption, I could not have said, and still cannot say, what it was that I actually thought. There were no particular questions that I asked myself; there were no special objects upon which I directed my mind; there was only a formless and aimless intellectual disturbance, as if I were wrestling with a fog.

I know now that this is what always happens when I am in the early stages of work on a problem. Until the problem has gone a long way towards being solved, I do not know what it is; all I am conscious of is this vague perturbation of mind, this sense of being worried about I cannot say what. I know now that the problems of my life's work were taking, deep down inside me, their first embryonic shape. But any one who observed me must have thought, as my elders did think, that I had fallen into a habit of loafing, and lost the alertness and quickness of wit that had been so noticeable in my early childhood. My only defence against this opinion, since I did not know and therefore could not explain what was happening to me, was to cover these fits of abstraction with some bodily activity, trifling enough not to distract my attention from my inward wrestling. I was a neat-fingered boy, skilful at making all sorts of things; active in walking, bicycling, or rowing, and thoroughly practised in sailing a boat. So when the fit was upon me I would set myself to make something quite uninteresting, like a regiment of paper men, or wander aimlessly in the woods or on the mountains, or sail all day in a dead calm. It was painful to be laughed at for playing with paper men; but the alternative, to explain why I did it, was impossible.

Whether it was this growing idleness that made my father send me to school, I am not sure. In any case he was too poor to pay for it himself, and my school bills (and later my Oxford bills) were paid by the generosity of a rich friend. Thus, at thirteen, I was put into a preparatory school with the aim of competing for a scholarship, and became acquainted with the treadmill on which middle-class boys in this country earn their own living by competitive examination, beginning at an age when their working-class fellow

children are debarred by law from exposing themselves in the labour market. My father's friend would,
I am sure, as willingly have paid two hundred pounds
a year for me as one; but to myself at least it was a
point of honour that I should win scholarships, if
only to justify the spending upon me of all that money;
and, even had it not been, the specialism which is one
chief vice of English education would not have spared
me. The ghost of a silly seventeenth-century squabble
still haunts our classrooms, infecting teachers and
pupils with the lunatic idea that studies must be either
'classical' or 'modern'. I was equally well fitted to
specialize in Greek and Latin, or in modern history
and languages (I spoke and read French and German
almost as easily as English), or in the natural sciences;
and nothing would have afforded my mind its proper
nourishment except to study equally all three; but
my father's teaching had given me a good deal more
Greek and Latin than most boys of my age possessed;
and since I had to specialize in something I specialized
in these and became a 'classical' scholar.

SPRING FROST

II

SPRING FROST

In that capacity I went on, a year later, to Rugby; a school which then had a high reputation, owing (as I found out in time) to the genius of one first-rate teacher, Robert Whitelaw, a man who touched nothing that he did not adorn. Because one of my five years there was spent in his form, it would be untrue to say that my time at Rugby was altogether wasted. And there were other things. I was in the Sixth Form for three years and head of my house for two; thus for the first time I tasted the pleasure of doing administrative work, and learnt once for all how to do it. In addition to Whitelaw, whose obviously sincere assumption that you knew as much as he did stimulated his pupils to incredible feats, I worked for a time under one other good teacher, C. P. Hastings, from whom I learnt a good deal of modern history. Among those of the other masters who did not have to teach me I made a few good friends; and with my contemporaries my relations were always of the happiest.

These were benefits conferred by the school itself: others I obtained rather in spite of it. I discovered Bach, learned to play the violin, studied harmony and counterpoint and orchestration, and composed a great deal of trash. I taught myself to read Dante and made the acquaintance of many other poets, in various languages, hitherto unknown to me. These unauthorized readings (for which, in summer time, I used to perch in a willow-tree overhanging the Avon) are my happiest recollection of Rugby; but not my most vivid.

That description must apply to the pigsty conditions of our daily life and the smell of filth constantly in our nostrils. Second to that comes the frightful boredom of being taught things (and things which ought to have been frightfully interesting) by weary, absent-minded or incompetent masters; then the torment of living by a time-table expressly devised to fill up the day with scraps and snippets of occupation in such a manner that no one could get down to a job of work and make something of it, and, in particular, devised to prevent one from doing that 'thinking' in which, long ago, I had recognized my own vocation.

Nor did I get any compensating satisfaction out of the organized games which constituted the real religion of the school; for at football in my first year I suffered an injury to the knee which the surgery of those days rendered incurable. This was a crucial point in my school life. The orthodox theory of public-school athletics is that they distract the adolescent from sex. They do not do that; but they give him a most necessary outlet for the energies he is not allowed to use in the class-room. Apart from a few eccentrics like Whitelaw, the public school masters of my acquaintance were like the schoolmaster in the *Dunciad*:

> Plac'd at the door of learning, youth to guide,
> We never suffer it to stand too wide.

The boys were nothing if not teachable. They soon saw that any exhibition of interest in their studies was a sure way to get themselves disliked, not by their contemporaries, but by the masters; and they were not long in acquiring that pose of boredom towards learning and everything connected with it which is notoriously part of the English public school man's character. But they must have some compensation for their frustrated and inhibited intellects; and this they got in athletics, where nobody minds how hard you work, and the triumphs of the football field make amends for the miseries of the class-room. If I had retained the use of my limbs I should no doubt have become an athlete and stopped worrying my head about the crack of that door and what was hidden behind it. As it was, I could not reconcile myself to the starvation imposed on me by the teaching to which I was subjected; and as time went on I learnt to devote my time more and more to music and to reading in subjects of my own choice like medieval Italian history or the early French poets, not because I preferred them to Thucydides and Catullus, but because I could work at them unhampered by masters.

These habits were not undiscovered, and I became a rebel, more or less declared, against the whole system of teaching. I did not rebel against the disciplinary system, and with my housemaster (my immediate superior in the disciplinary hierarchy) I remained on excellent terms; I did not even neglect my work to the extent of incurring punishment for idleness; but my masters were quite able to discern the difference between my abilities and my performance, and were

justifiably annoyed by it; especially, I seemed to
notice, when they had to send up my compositions,
or as we called them 'copies', to the headmaster for
distinction. I could not prevent that from happening;
for my plan was ca' canny, not sabotage, and I would
not wilfully write bad 'copies'. But I could and did
refuse to enter for the prizes which decorated the
career of a good boy. To make this refusal more
pointed, I would enter now and then for a prize that
had nothing to do with my proper subjects of study:
one for English literature, which I remember with
gratitude because it introduced me to Dryden, one for
astronomy, which entailed many nights with the four-
inch equatorial and the transit instrument in the
school observatory, one for musical theory and compo-
sition, and one (which I failed to win) for reading
aloud.

The much-tried form-master of the Upper Bench
made a bid for revenge when I proposed to enter for
a scholarship at Oxford. He refused me leave to sit.
I had no chance of winning one, he said, and he did
not wish to have the school disgraced. I reported this
to my father, who was an irascible man and wrote to
the headmaster. My first choice was University College; to give myself another chance, I entered for a
second 'group' of colleges, and thus spent two successive weeks inhabiting college rooms in Oxford. The
first examination I took very seriously; in the second
I decided to enjoy myself, and behaved disgracefully.
In the verse paper I wrote neither Latin nor Greek,
but the English verses permitted to those whose clas-

sics were shaky. In the 'general' paper I spent my whole time answering a question about Turner and another about Mozart; and what boyish nonsense I put into my essay I dare not try to recollect. But at the *viva voce* examination they asked me what I should do if I had to choose between the best scholarship in that group and an inferior one at University; and when I answered that University was my father's College and that I should go there if I was offered any scholarship at all, they did not seem like men who thought the worse of me.

But my form-master had the last word. There was a leaving exhibition confined to natives of my home county; and I told him, as the proper person, that I wished to enter for it. Time went by and nothing happened; and at last I spoke of it again. He answered that he had forgotten to send in my name and that it was now too late. So in due course that exhibition was announced with the formula 'no candidate'. This time I did not protest.

To apportion blame for mishaps is seldom worth doing. If my five years at Rugby were mainly waste, the fault lies partly with the obvious faults of the English public-school system; partly with Rugby as a bad example of that system, though among its faults I do not reckon the institution of fagging or that of government by members of the sixth form, both of which I count as virtues; partly with my father, who gave me an adult scholar's attitude towards learning while I was still a child, realizing, as I now think, what the results would be, but judging the game worth the candle; and partly with myself, for being a conceited puppy and an opinionated prig.

To show that I mean these epithets seriously, I will describe one incident of the feud between that form-master and myself. Reading to his form a note by some modern scholar, as it might be Jebb, on a passage in a Greek text, he came to the word floret, and said 'Floret? I don't believe there is such a word. Has any of you heard of it?' All the rest held their tongues, and so should I have done if I had learnt to be a proper schoolboy; but something inside me whispered 'for God's sake, speak up and put an end to this silly game of hide-and-seek'; and I said 'It means one of the little things that make up a flower of the order *compositae*; I expect he got it from Browning's description of the sunflower, "with ray-like florets round a disk-like face".' And I still remember, with bitter shame, the contemptuous tone in which I said it, and the disconcerted face with which the poor man complimented me on my learning.

Going up to Oxford was like being let out of prison. In those days, before the anthology habit infected Classical Moderations, a candidate for honours was expected to read Homer, Vergil, Demosthenes, and the speeches of Cicero more or less entire, in addition to a special study of other texts, among which I chose Lucretius, Theocritus, and the *Agamemnon*. This was not only leading a horse to the water, but (hardly less important) leaving him there. The happy beast could swill and booze Homer until the world contained no Homer that he had not read. After long years on a

ration of twenty drops a day, nicely medicated from
a form-master's fad-bottle, I drank with open throat.
One hour a week I had to spend showing compositions to my tutor; and there were a few lectures which
he had advised me to attend: otherwise my time was
my own. Nor were these exceptions very serious. If
I had shut myself up in my rooms for a week together,
to do some work of my own choosing, my tutor would
only have passed it off, when I emerged very apolo-
getic, with an erudite but good-humoured joke. In
short, I had come to a place where, even if it was not
actually assumed that one had an adult attitude towards learning, at any rate one was not penalized for
having such an attitude; and all I had to do was to
forget my school life and let myself go.

Yet it was not quite so simple as that. The ill effects
of my school years could not be removed by a mere
change of environment. My long-baulked craving for
knowledge was now almost morbid. I could think of
nothing else. Perched in my tower in the garden
quadrangle of University College, I read all day and
most of the night. All the good easy social life that
was going on around me I brushed aside. Even my
friendships were few. Long experience of hostility between myself and the system under which I lived had
made me cynical, suspicious, and eccentric; caring
little for my relations with my neighbours; quick to
take offence and not unready to give it. But, for all
that, there were many long walks in the country,
many idle afternoons on the river, many evenings
spent playing and hearing music, many nights talking

until dawn; and more than one lifelong friendship in the making.

When the time came to begin 'Greats' I found the same method at work. I had now two tutors, one in philosophy and one in ancient history, each demanding a weekly essay: but otherwise, apart from a little advice about lectures, I was perfectly free to arrange my own studies in my own way; and I used my freedom. When I was supposed to be working at ancient history I spent much time reading reports of excavations at Greek and Roman sites; one whole long vacation went in studying everything I could get hold of about ancient Sicily; in philosophy, where our studies were supposed to end with Kant, I managed to acquire a rough and sketchy, but first-hand, acquaintance with most of the chief writers, in English, French, German, and Italian, from that time down to the present, and once I spent several weeks reading Plato from end to end. I mention these things not in order to boast of my industry; they are a fleabite to what a very ordinary eighteenth-century student of my years would have done; but, because they were all done without the orders and mostly even without the knowledge of my tutors, as evidence of the extent to which I was left alone to work in peace. My contemporaries knew hardly more about these doings than my tutors: I was always too busy to join the societies at whose meetings undergraduates exhibited their wits and their learning to mutual admiration.

III

MINUTE PHILOSOPHERS

WHEN I began to read philosophy there in 1910, Oxford was still obsessed by what I will call the school of Green: a philosophical movement whose leader was Thomas Hill Green and whose other chief members were Francis Herbert Bradley, Bernard Bosanquet, William Wallace, and Robert Lewis Nettleship. No one has yet written the history of this movement, and I do not propose to attempt it here; but I cannot indicate the problems which I found confronting me without a few remarks on the subject.

The philosophical tendencies common to this school were described by its contemporary opponents as Hegelianism. This title was repudiated by the school itself, and rightly. Their philosophy, so far as they had one single philosophy, was a continuation and criticism of the indigenous English and Scottish philosophies of the middle nineteenth century. It is true that, unlike most of their compatriots, they had some knowledge of Hegel, and a good deal more of Kant. The fact of their having this knowledge was used by their opponents, more through ignorance than through deliberate dishonesty, to discredit them in the eyes of a public always contemptuous of foreigners. Green had read Hegel in youth, but rejected him in middle age; the philosophy he was working out when his early death interrupted him is best described, if a brief description is needed, as a reply to Herbert

Spencer by a profound student of Hume. Bradley, who knew enough of Hegel to be certain that he disagreed with his cardinal doctrines, and said so, published a series of books whose purpose is written plainly upon them: they are criticisms of Mill's logic, Bain's psychology, and Mansel's metaphysics by a man whose mind was the most deeply critical that European philosophy has produced since Hume, and whose intention, like that of Locke, was to make a bonfire of rubbish.

This movement never in any sense dominated philosophical thought and teaching in Oxford. In its most flourishing period it comprised only a few young men. Their views were always regarded with suspicion by the most part of their colleagues; and not one of them enjoyed in Oxford a long life of teaching. T. H. Green died at forty-six in 1882, after being a professor for four years. R. L. Nettleship, who was placed in the second class in 'Greats' because he 'handed out' Green's views to the examiners, perished in the Alps, at the same age, in 1892. Bosanquet, after teaching in Oxford for eleven years, left it for good in 1881, at thirty-three. Wallace was killed in an accident at fifty-three, in 1897. Bradley, though he lived in Oxford down to his death in 1924, never taught there and never sought in any way to propagate his philosophy by personal contacts. He lived a very retired life; although I lived within a few hundred yards of him for sixteen years, I never to my knowledge set eyes on him.

The real strength of the movement was outside

Oxford. The 'Greats' school was not meant as a training for professional scholars and philosophers; it was meant as a training for public life in the Church, at the Bar, in the Civil Service, and in Parliament. The school of Green sent out into public life a stream of ex-pupils who carried with them the conviction that philosophy, and in particular the philosophy they had learnt at Oxford, was an important thing, and that their vocation was to put it into practice. This conviction was common to politicians so diverse in their creeds as Asquith and Milner, churchmen like Gore and Scott Holland, social reformers like Arnold Toynbee, and a host of other public men whose names it would be tedious to repeat. Through this effect on the minds of its pupils, the philosophy of Green's school might be found, from about 1880 to about 1910, penetrating and fertilizing every part of the national life.[1]

Since the philosophy of Green's school had never been predominant among teachers, the hostility to it which was so prevalent in 1910 can hardly be called a reaction. It would be truer to describe it as representing the old academic tradition, labouring to eradicate what it had always regarded as a growth foreign to its own nature. The old stock was shooting up from below the graft, the scion dying back, and the tree reverting to its original state.

[1] The only attempt yet made to trace the history of this penetration is that of Dr. Klaus Dockhorn, *Die Staatsphilosophie des englischen Idealismus: ihre Lehre und Wirkung* (Cologne 1937), part ii.

There were still among the philosophers a few representatives of the original movement. The best of them were J. A. Smith, who had been a pupil of Nettleship, and H. H. Joachim, a close personal friend of Bradley. Each of these later became an intimate and beloved friend of my own, and I cannot think of either without gratitude and admiration;[1] but this must not prevent me from saying that they failed to avert the collapse of the school to which they belonged. The way in which this could have been done was by expounding and developing the doctrines of that school in a series of books addressed to the general public; but between them they produced only one such book, Joachim's essay on *The Nature of Truth*, whose success with the public showed unmistakably, but in vain, the demand that existed for such things. Yet, if they did not satisfy this demand, it was only because they could not. They were the *epigoni* of a great movement; and like all *epigoni* they felt that what needed to be said had been said, and need not be repeated. Often I urged them to write; and always I found that my urging was met by no corresponding impulse within themselves. They could not write, because they did not feel that they had anything to say.

The game was thus left in the hands of their opponents. These called themselves 'realists',[2] and undertook the task of discrediting the entire work of

[1] And in Joachim's case with mourning. He died soon after this chapter was written.

[2] Thomas Case (1844–1925), a leading Oxford opponent of Green's school, had written books advocating 'realism', by that name, from the 1870's onwards.

Green's school, which they described comprehensively as 'idealism' (another title explicitly repudiated by Bradley, the greatest philosopher of the school). When I say that Green's school at this time obsessed Oxford philosophy, what I mean is that the work of that school presented itself to most Oxford philosophers as something which had to be destroyed, and in destroying which they would be discharging their first duty to their subject. The question what positive views they themselves held was of secondary importance.

The leader of this school was John Cook Wilson, professor of logic. He was a fiery, pugnacious little man with a passion for controversy and an instinctive eye for its tactics; more important, an inspiring teacher, whose enthusiasm for philosophical thought I still remember with admiration and gratitude. He, too, refrained from publication; and he once explained to me his reasons. 'I rewrite, on average, one third of my logic lectures every year', said he. 'That means I'm constantly changing my mind about every point in the subject. If I published, every book I wrote would betray a change of mind since writing the last. Now, if you let the public know that you change your mind, they will never take you seriously. Therefore it is best never to publish at all.' Whether he thought that by not publishing he deceived the public into thinking that he never changed his mind, and whether he regarded this as a good thing to do, even though the public remained ignorant what his mind was, or whether he had a mind at all, I did not ask; probably because I already knew that there are two reasons why people refrain from writing books: either they are conscious that they have nothing to say, or they are conscious that they are unable to say it; and that if they give any other reason than these it is to throw dust in other people's eyes or their own.

Other sayings were more to his credit. Commenting on something I had written about Plato's *Sophist*, and led thereby to hold forth about the kind of people who disseminate error, he said, 'there are two kinds of damn fool: there are damn silly fools like X, and damn clever fools like Y; and if you're going to be a damn fool you'd much better be a damn silly one.' I am sorry I cannot think myself justified in naming the eminent contemporary philosophers whom I have called X and Y.

After Cook Wilson, the most important members of the 'realist' school were his followers H. A. Prichard and H. W. B. Joseph. Prichard was an extremely acute and pertinacious thinker, who if common report was right had on occasion been more leader than follower to Cook Wilson. At the time I speak of he had just published a book entitled *Kant's Theory of Knowledge*, in which the argument of the 'Aesthetic' and 'Analytic' portions of the *Critique of Pure Reason* were attacked from a 'realist' point of view. He used to lecture on the theories of knowledge preceding Kant's, from Descartes onward, showing how 'idealist' tendencies had been at work throughout the seventeenth and eighteenth centuries, and refuting all the theories which they had infected. Joseph, author of an *Introduction to Logic* in which a position not unlike

Cook Wilson's was taken up, lectured on Plato's *Republic*, and would hardly have repudiated the name of Platonist: for he regarded Plato as right in many at least of his views, and especially on those points with respect to which the 'idealists' were wrong. Subsequently, Prichard and Joseph tended increasingly to diverge. Prichard, developing his extraordinary gift for destructive criticism, by degrees destroyed not only the 'idealism' he at first set out to destroy but the 'realism' in whose interest he set out to destroy it, and described a path converging visibly, as years went by, with the zero-line of complete scepticism. In Joseph's case this scepticism was masked by a progressive tendency to accept Plato's doctrines as substantially true. But the scepticism was nevertheless there; or so it seemed to his pupils, one of whom once said to me, 'if the Archangel Gabriel told you what Mr. Joseph really thought about something, and you served it up to him in an essay, I'm perfectly sure he would prove to you that it was wrong'.

IV

INCLINATION OF A SAPLING

MY own tutor E. F. Carritt was another prominent member of the 'realist' school, and sent me to lectures with Cook Wilson and the rest. I was thus thoroughly indoctrinated with its principles and methods. But though I called myself a 'realist', it was not without some reservations. An important document of the school, or rather of the parallel and more or less allied school at Cambridge, was G. E. Moore's recently published article called 'The Refutation of Idealism'. This purported to be a criticism of Berkeley. Now the position actually criticized in that article is not Berkeley's position; indeed, in certain important respects it is the exact position which Berkeley was controverting. In order to see this, I had only to open the article and Berkeley's text and compare them. The same thing happened with the attacks on Bradley made in Cook Wilson's logic lectures. I am sure that few of his audience took much trouble about comparing these with Bradley's text and asking how far they tallied with it. But I did; and I found that he constantly criticized Bradley for views which were not Bradley's.

I do not apologize for having felt, when young, the diffidence of youth. At forty, I should not have hesitated for a moment, if I had been attached to a school of thought whose leaders I had convicted of errors so gross on matters of fact so important, to break the attachment. At twenty-two or twenty-three I distinguished and qualified. I argued that the 'realists' professed philosophy, not history; that their business, strictly as philosophical critics, was to show whether a certain doctrine were sound or unsound, and that this they had done, on the present occasion, admirably; that their historical blunders on the question whether a certain author held that doctrine, however distressing to myself, did not affect the philosophical issue; and that I was logically bound to remain a 'realist' until I had satisfied myself either that the positive doctrines of the school were false, or that its critical methods were unsound.

These questions I did not answer until after I had taken my degree and begun to work as a teacher of philosophy. It then became clear to me, as I tried to settle in my own mind how the methods and doctrines of my 'realist' colleagues were related, that Cook Wilson's positive teaching was incapable of resisting attack by his own critical methods. If the positive teaching and the critical methods had been logically connected, that would have been fatal to both of them; but there might be no such connexion. The positive teaching might be mistaken, and the critical methods valid, or *vice versa*. To choose between these three alternatives was the problem still occupying my mind in 1914, when our academic life was broken up by war.

Meanwhile I had been half unconsciously preparing a flank attack on the same problem. When I became a teacher of philosophy I did not abandon my historical and archaeological studies. Every summer

I spent serving on the staff of some large excavation, and from 1913 onwards directing excavations of my own. This became one of the chief pleasures of my life. I had learnt how to manage schoolboys; now I had to manage labourers, to keep them well and happy, to understand their approach to our common task and help them to understand mine. At the same time I found myself experimenting in a laboratory of knowledge; at first asking myself a quite vague question, such as: 'was there a Flavian occupation on this site?' then dividing that question into various heads and putting the first in some such form as this: 'are these Flavian sherds and coins mere strays, or were they deposited in the period to which they belong?' and then considering all the possible ways in which light could be thrown on this new question, and putting them into practice one by one, until at last I could say, 'There was a Flavian occupation; an earth and timber fort of such and such plan was built here in the year $a \pm b$ and abandoned for such and such reasons in the year $x \pm y$.' Experience soon taught me that under these laboratory conditions one found out nothing at all except in answer to a question; and not a vague question either, but a definite one. That when one dug saying merely, 'Let us see what there is here', one learnt nothing, except casually in so far as casual questions arose in one's mind while digging: 'Is that black stuff peat or occupation-soil? Is that a potsherd under your foot? Are those loose stones a ruined wall?' That what one learnt depended not merely on what turned up in one's trenches but also on what questions one was asking: so that a man who was asking questions of one kind learnt one kind of thing from a piece of digging which to another man revealed something different, to a third something illusory, and to a fourth nothing at all.

Here I was only rediscovering for myself, in the practice of historical research, principles which Bacon and Descartes had stated, three hundred years earlier, in connexion with the natural sciences. Each of them had said very plainly that knowledge comes only by answering questions, and that these questions must be the right questions and asked in the right order. And I had often read the works in which they said it; but I did not understand them until I had found the same thing out for myself.

The Oxford 'realists' talked as if knowing were a simple 'intuiting' or a simple 'apprehending' of some 'reality'. At Cambridge, Moore expressed, as I thought, the same conception when he spoke of the 'transparency' of the act of knowing; so did Alexander, at Manchester, when he described knowing as the simple 'compresence' of two things, one of which was a mind. What all these 'realists' were saying, I thought, was that the condition of a knowing mind is not indeed a passive condition, for it is actively engaged in knowing; but a 'simple' condition, one in which there are no complexities or diversities, nothing except just the knowing. They granted that a man who wanted to know something might have to work, in ways that might be very complicated, in order to 'put himself in a position' from which it could be 'apprehended';

but once the position had been attained there was nothing for him to do but 'apprehend' it, or perhaps fail to 'apprehend' it.

This doctrine, which was rendered plausible by choosing as examples of knowledge statements like 'this is a red rose', 'my hand is resting on the table', where familiarity with the mental operations involved has bred not so much contempt as oblivion, was quite incompatible with what I had learned in my 'laboratory' of historical thought. The questioning activity, as I called it, was not an activity of achieving compresence with, or apprehension of, something; it was not preliminary to the act of knowing; it was one half (the other half being answering the question) of an act which in its totality was knowing.

I have tried to state the point as it appeared to me at the time. I was well enough trained in 'realist' methods to know exactly what a 'realist' would have said in answer to my statement of it. But Cook Wilson himself had said to me once: 'I will say one thing about you: you can see the obvious.' And it was obvious to me that such an answer would have been no more than an attempt to argue the hind leg off a donkey.

In my philosophical teaching I was working on a line which ultimately converged with this. From the first, I decided that one thing which Oxford philosophy needed was a background (at the time, I conceived it as merely that) of sound scholarship: such a habit of mind as would make it impossible for an Oxford-trained student to be deceived by Moore's 'refutation' of Berkeley or Cook Wilson's of Bradley. I therefore taught my pupils, more by example than by precept, that they must never accept any criticism of anybody's philosophy which they might hear or read without satisfying themselves by first-hand study that this was the philosophy he actually expounded; that they must always defer any criticism of their own until they were absolutely sure they understood the text they were criticizing; and that if the postponement was *sine die* it did not greatly matter. This did not as yet involve any attack upon the 'realists'' critical methods. When my pupils came to me armed with grotesquely irrelevant refutations of (say) Kant's ethical theory, and told me they came out of So-and-so's lectures, it was all one to me whether the irrelevance came from their misrepresenting So-and-so, or from So-and-so's misrepresenting Kant: my move was to reach for a book with the words, 'Let us see whether that is what Kant really said'.

In lecturing, I adopted a similar procedure. I had become something of a specialist in Aristotle, and the first lectures I gave were on the *De Anima*. My plan was to concentrate on the question, 'What is Aristotle saying and what does he mean by it?' and to forgo, however alluring it might be, the further question 'Is it true?' What I wanted was to train my audience in the scholarly approach to a philosophical text, leaving on one side, as sufficiently provided for by other teachers, the further business of criticizing its doctrine.

By the time war broke out in 1914 and put a stop to

all this, I had not indeed answered to my own satisfaction the threefold question stated earlier in this chapter; but I had made good progress with what I have called the flank attack upon it. I had made myself an expert in a certain kind of research, and had found out how to use it as a laboratory for testing epistemological theories. I had also established and perfected what, had I been a great artist, might have been called my 'early manner' in philosophical teaching. Working simultaneously along these two lines, I could see them tending to converge in an attack on 'realism' as a philosophy which erred through neglecting history. If I had thought it possible to forewarn the 'realists' of this attack, I should have said, 'You must pay more attention to history. Your positive doctrines about knowledge are incompatible with what happens, according to my own experience, in historical research; and your critical methods are misused on doctrines which in historical fact were never held by those to whom you ascribe them.'

A great deal of hard thinking was needed, before the vague dissatisfaction which I might have expressed in some such words as these could be focused into a clear issue. And I am not sure that I could ever so have focused it, but for the interruption of my academic life by the war. A man whose mind is always being stirred up by philosophical teaching can hardly be expected to achieve the calm, the inner silence, which is one condition of philosophical thinking.

V

QUESTION AND ANSWER

A YEAR or two after the outbreak of war, I was living in London and working with a section of the Admiralty Intelligence Division in the rooms of the Royal Geographical Society. Every day I walked across Kensington Gardens and past the Albert Memorial. The Albert Memorial began by degrees to obsess me. Like Wordsworth's Leech-gatherer, it took on a strange air of significance; it seemed

> Like one whom I had met with in a dream;
> Or like a man from some far region sent,
> To give me human strength, by apt admonishment.

Everything about it was visibly mis-shapen, corrupt, crawling, verminous; for a time I could not bear to look at it, and passed with averted eyes; recovering from this weakness, I forced myself to look, and to face day by day the question: a thing so obviously, so incontrovertibly, so indefensibly bad, why had Scott done it? To say that Scott was a bad architect was to burke the problem with a tautology; to say that there was no accounting for tastes was to evade it by *suggestio falsi*. What relation was there, I began to ask myself, between what he had done and what he had tried to do? Had he tried to produce a beautiful thing; a thing, I meant, which we should have thought beautiful? If so, he had of course failed. But had he perhaps been trying to produce something different? If so, he might possibly have succeeded. If I found the monument merely loathsome, was that perhaps my fault? Was I looking in it for qualities it did not possess, and either ignoring or despising those it did?

I will not try to describe everything I went through in what, for many months, continued to be my daily communings with the Albert Memorial. Of the various thoughts that came to me in those communings I will only state one: a further development of a thought already familiar to me.

My work in archaeology, as I have said, impressed upon me the importance of the 'questioning activity' in knowledge: and this made it impossible for me to rest contented with the intuitionist theory of knowledge favoured by the 'realists'. The effect of this on my logic was to bring about in my mind a revolt against the current logical theories of the time, a good deal like that revolt against the scholastic logic which was produced in the minds of Bacon and Descartes by reflection on the experience of scientific research, as that was taking new shape in the late sixteenth and early seventeenth centuries. The *Novum Organum* and the *Discours de la Méthode* began to have a new significance for me. They were the classical expressions of a principle in logic which I found it necessary to restate: the principle that a body of knowledge consists not of 'propositions', 'statements', 'judgements', or whatever name logicians use in order to designate assertive acts of thought (or what in those acts is asserted: for 'knowledge' means both the activity of knowing and what is known), but of these together with the questions they are meant to answer; and that a logic in which the answers are attended to and the questions neglected is a false logic.

I will try to indicate, briefly as the nature of this book requires (for it is an autobiography, not a work on logic), the way in which this notion developed in my mind as I reflected day by day upon the Albert Memorial. I know that what I am going to say is very controversial, and that almost any reader who is already something of a logician will violently disagree with it. But I shall make no attempt to forestall his criticisms. So far as he belongs to any logical school now existing, I think I know already what they will be, and it is because I am not convinced by them that I am writing this chapter. I shall not use the word 'judgement', like the so-called 'idealistic' logicians, or Cook Wilson's word 'statement': the thing denoted by these words I shall call a 'proposition': so that this word will always in this chapter denote a logical, not a linguistic, entity.

I began by observing that you cannot find out what a man means by simply studying his spoken or written statements, even though he has spoken or written with perfect command of language and perfectly truthful intention. In order to find out his meaning you must also know what the question was (a question in his own mind, and presumed by him to be in yours) to which the thing he has said or written was meant as an answer.

It must be understood that question and answer, as I conceived them, were strictly correlative. A proposition was not an answer, or at any rate could not be the right answer, to any question which might have been answered otherwise. A highly detailed and particularized proposition must be the answer, not to a vague and generalized question, but to a question as detailed and particularized as itself. For example, if my car will not go, I may spend an hour searching for the cause of its failure. If, during this hour, I take out number one plug, lay it on the engine, turn the starting-handle, and watch for a spark, my observation 'number one plug is all right' is an answer not to the question, 'Why won't my car go?' but to the question, 'Is it because number one plug is not sparking that my car won't go?' Any one of the various experiments I make during the hour will be the finding of an answer to some such detailed and particularized question. The question, 'Why won't my car go?' is only a kind of summary of all these taken together. It is not a separate question asked at a separate time, nor is it a sustained question which I continue to ask for the whole hour together. Consequently, when I say 'Number one plug is all right', this observation does not record one more failure to answer the hour-long question, 'What is wrong with my car?' It records a success in answering the three-minutes-long question, 'Is the stoppage due to failure in number one plug?'

In passing, I will note (what I shall return to later on) that this principle of correlativity between question and answer disposes of a good deal of clap-trap. People will speak of a savage as 'confronted by the eternal problem of obtaining food'. But what really confronts him is the problem, quite transitory like all things human, of spearing this fish, or digging up this root, or finding blackberries in this wood.

My next step was to apply this principle to the idea of contradiction. The current logic maintained that two propositions might, simply as propositions, contradict one another, and that by examining them simply as propositions you could find out whether they did so or not. This I denied. If you cannot tell what a proposition means unless you know what question it is meant to answer, you will mistake its meaning if you make a mistake about that question. One symptom of mistaking the meaning of a proposition is thinking that it contradicts another proposition which in fact it does not contradict. No two propositions, I saw, can contradict one another unless they are answers to the same question. It is therefore impossible to say of a man, 'I do not know what the question is which he is trying to answer, but I can see that he is contradicting himself'.

The same principle applied to the idea of truth. If the meaning of a proposition is relative to the question it answers, its truth must be relative to the same thing. Meaning, agreement and contradiction, truth and falsehood, none of these belonged to propositions in their own right, propositions by themselves; they belonged only to propositions as the answers to questions: each proposition answering a question strictly correlative to itself.

Here I parted company with what I called propositional logic, and its offspring the generally recognized theories of truth. According to propositional logic (under which denomination I include the so-called 'traditional' logic, the 'idealistic' logic of the eighteenth and nineteenth centuries, and the 'symbolic' logic of the nineteenth and twentieth), truth or falsehood, which are what logic is chiefly concerned with, belongs to propositions as such. This doctrine was often expressed by calling the proposition the 'unit of thought', meaning that if you divide it up into parts such as subject, copula, predicate, any of these parts taken singly is not a complete thought, that is, not capable of being true or false.

It seemed to me that this doctrine was a mistake due to the early partnership between logic and grammar. The logician's proposition seemed to me a kind of ghostly double of the grammarian's sentence, just as in primitive speculation about the mind people imagine minds as ghostly doubles of bodies. Grammar recognizes a form of discourse called the sentence, and among sentences, as well as other kinds which serve as the verbal expressions of questions, commands, &c., one kind which express statements. In grammatical phraseology, these are indicative sentences; and logicians have almost always tried to conceive the 'unit of thought', or that which is either true or false, as a kind of logical 'soul' whose linguistic 'body' is the indicative sentence.

This attempt to correlate the logical proposition with the grammatical indicative sentence has never been altogether satisfactory. There have always been people who saw that the true 'unit of thought' was not the proposition but something more complex in which the proposition served as answer to a question. Not only Bacon and Descartes, but Plato and Kant, come to mind as examples. When Plato described thinking as a 'dialogue of the soul with itself', he meant (as we know from his own dialogues) that it was a process of question and answer, and that of these two elements the primacy belongs to the questioning activity, the Socrates within us. When Kant said that it takes a wise man to know what questions he can reasonably ask, he was in effect repudiating a merely propositional logic and demanding a logic of question and answer.

Even apart from this, however, logic has never been able to assert a *de facto* one-one relation between propositions and indicative sentences. It has always maintained that the words actually used by a man on a given occasion in order to express his thought may be 'elliptical' or 'pleonastic' or in some other way not quite in accordance with the rule that one sentence should express one proposition. It is generally held, again, that indicative sentences in a work of fiction, professing to be that and nothing more, do not express propositions. But when these and other qualifications have been made, this can be described as the central doctrine of propositional logic: that there is, or ought to be, or in a well-constructed and well-used language would be,[1] a one-one correspondence between pro-

---

[1] Hence that numerous and frightful offspring of propositional logic out of illiteracy, the various attempts at a 'logical language', beginning with the pedantry of the text-books about 'reducing

positions and indicative sentences, every indicative sentence expressing a proposition, and a proposition being defined as the unit of thought, or that which is true or false.

This is the doctrine which is presupposed by all the various well-known theories of truth. One school of thought holds that a proposition is either true or false simply in itself, trueness or falseness being qualities of propositions. Another school holds that to call it true or false is to assert a relation of 'correspondence' or 'non-correspondence' between it and something not a proposition, some 'state of things' or 'fact'. A third holds that to call it true or false is to assert a relation between it and other propositions with which it 'coheres' or fails to 'cohere'. And, since in those days there were pragmatists, a fourth school should be mentioned, holding (at least according to some of their pronouncements) that to call a proposition true or false is to assert the utility or inutility of believing it.

All these theories of truth I denied. This was not very original of me; any one could see, after reading Joachim's *Nature of Truth*, that they were all open to fatal objections. My reason for denying them, however, was not that they were severally open to objections, but that they all presupposed what I have called the principle of propositional logic; and this principle I denied altogether.

For a logic of propositions I wanted to substitute

a proposition to logical form', and ending, for the present, in the typographical jargon of *Principia Mathematica*.

what I called a logic of question and answer. It seemed to me that truth, if that meant the kind of thing which I was accustomed to pursue in my ordinary work as a philosopher or historian—truth in the sense in which a philosophical theory or an historical narrative is called true, which seemed to me the proper sense of the word—was something that belonged not to any single proposition, nor even, as the coherence-theorists maintained, to a complex of propositions taken together; but to a complex consisting of questions and answers. The structure of this complex had, of course, never been studied by propositional logic; but with help from Bacon, Descartes, and others I could hazard a few statements about it. Each question and each answer in a given complex had to be relevant or appropriate, had to 'belong' both to the whole and to the place it occupied in the whole. Each question had to 'arise'; there must be that about it whose absence we condemn when we refuse to answer a question on the ground that it 'doesn't arise'. Each answer must be 'the right' answer to the question it professes to answer.

By 'right' I do not mean 'true'. The 'right' answer to a question is the answer which enables us to get ahead with the process of questioning and answering. Cases are quite common in which the 'right' answer to a question is 'false'; for example, cases in which a thinker is following a false scent, either inadvertently or in order to construct a *reductio ad absurdum*. Thus, when Socrates asks (Plato, *Republic*, 333 B) whether as your partner in a game of draughts you would prefer to have a just man or a man who knows how to play draughts, the answer which Polemarchus gives—'a man who knows how to play draughts'—is the right answer. It is 'false', because it presupposes that justice and ability to play draughts are comparable, each of them being a 'craft', or specialized form of skill. But it is 'right', because it constitutes a link, and a sound one, in the chain of questions and answers by which the falseness of that presupposition is made manifest.

What is ordinarily meant when a proposition is called 'true', I thought, was this: (*a*) the proposition belongs to a question-and-answer complex which as a whole is 'true' in the proper sense of the word; (*b*) within this complex it is an answer to a certain question; (*c*) the question is what we ordinarily call a sensible or intelligent question, not a silly one, or in my terminology it 'arises'; (*d*) the proposition is the 'right' answer to that question.

If this is what is meant by calling a proposition 'true', it follows not only that you cannot tell whether a proposition is 'true' or 'false' until you know what question it was intended to answer, but also that a proposition which in fact is 'true' can always be thought 'false' by any one who takes the trouble to excogitate a question to which it would have been the wrong answer, and convinces himself that this was the question it was meant to answer. And a proposition which in fact is significant can always be thought meaningless by any one who convinces himself that it was intended as an answer to a question which, if it had really been intended to answer it, it would not have answered at all, either rightly or wrongly. Whether a given proposition is true or false, significant or meaningless, depends on what question it was meant to answer; and any one who wishes to know whether a given proposition is true or false, significant or meaningless, must find out what question it was meant to answer.

Now, the question 'To what question did So-and-so intend this proposition for an answer?' is an historical question, and therefore cannot be settled except by historical methods. When So-and-so wrote in a distant past, it is generally a very difficult one, because writers (at any rate good writers) always write for their contemporaries, and in particular for those who are 'likely to be interested', which means those who are already asking the question to which an answer is being offered; and consequently a writer very seldom explains what the question is that he is trying to answer. Later on, when he has become a 'classic' and his contemporaries are all long dead, the question has been forgotten; especially if the answer he gave was generally acknowledged to be the right answer; for in that case people stopped asking the question, and began asking the question that next arose. So the question asked by the original writer can only be reconstructed historically, often not without the exercise of considerable historical skill.

''Sblood!' says Hamlet, 'do you think I am easier to be played on than a pipe?' Those eminent philosophers, Rosencrantz and Guildenstern, think *tout bonnement* that they can discover what the *Parmenides* is about by merely reading it; but if you took them to the south gate of Housesteads and said, 'Please distinguish the various periods of construction here, and explain what purpose the builders of each period had in mind', they would protest 'Believe me, I cannot'. Do they think the *Parmenides* is easier to understand than a rotten little Roman fort? 'Sblood!

It follows, too, and this is what especially struck me at the time, that whereas no two propositions can be in themselves mutually contradictory, there are many cases in which one and the same pair of propositions are capable of being thought either that or the opposite, according as the questions they were meant to answer are reconstructed in one way or in another. For example, metaphysicians have been heard to say 'the world is both one and many'; and critics have not been wanting who were stupid enough to accuse them of contradicting themselves, on the abstractly logical ground that 'the world is one' and 'the world is many' are mutually contradictory propositions. A great deal of the popular dislike of metaphysics is based on grounds of this sort, and is ultimately due to critics who, as we say, did not know what the men they criticized were talking about; that is, did not know what questions their talk was intended to answer; but, with the ordinary malevolence of the idle against the industrious, the ignorant against the learned, the fool against the wise man, wished to have it believed that they were talking nonsense.

Suppose, instead of talking about the world, the

metaphysician were talking about the contents of a small mahogany box with a sliding top; and suppose he said, 'The contents of this box are both one thing and many things'. A stupid critic may think that he is offering two incompatible answers to a single question, 'Are the contents of this box one x or many x's?' But the critic has reconstructed the question wrong. There were two questions: (a) Are the contents of this box one set of chessmen or many sets? (b) Are the contents of this box one chessman or many chessmen?

There is no contradiction between saying that something, whether that something be the world or the contents of a box, is one, and saying that it is many. Contradiction would set in only if that something were said to be both one x and many x's. But in the original statement, whether about the world or about the chessmen, there was nothing about one x and many x's. That was foisted upon it by the critic. The contradiction of which the critic complains never existed in his victim's philosophy at all, until the critic planted it upon him, as he might have planted treasonable correspondence in his coat pockets; and with an equally laudable intention, to obtain a reward for denouncing him.

Thus, if a given doctrine D is criticized as self-contradictory because it is divisible into two parts E and F, where E contradicts F, the criticism is valid only if the critic has correctly reconstructed the questions to which E and F were given as answers. A critic who is aware of this condition will of course 'show his working' by stating to his readers the evidence on which he has concluded that the author criticized really did formulate his questions in such a way that E and F in his mouth were mutually contradictory. Failing that, a reader disinclined to work the problem out for himself will naturally assume the criticism to be sound or unsound according as he has found the critic to be, in a general way, a good historian or a bad one.

This enabled me to answer the question, left open (as I stated at the end of the preceding chapter) in 1914, whether the 'realists'' critical methods were sound. The answer could only be that they were not. For the 'realists'' chief, and in the last resort, it seemed to me, only method was to analyse the position criticized into various propositions, and detect contradictions between these. Following as they did the rules of propositional logic, it never occurred to them that those contradictions might be the fruit of their own historical errors as to the questions which their victims had been trying to answer. There was also a chance that they might not be; but, after what I already knew about the 'realists'' attitude towards history, the odds seemed to me against it. In any case, so long as the possibility existed, the methods were vicious.

All this, during my spare time in 1917, I wrote out at considerable length, with a great many applications and illustrations, in a book called *Truth and Contradiction*. I went so far as to offer it to a publisher, but was told that the times were hopelessly bad for a book of that kind, and that I had better keep it for the present. The publisher was right on both points. Not only were the times unpropitious, but I was still a beginner in the art of writing books. I had only published one. It was called *Religion and Philosophy*, and was published in 1916. It had been written some years earlier, in order to tidy up and put behind me a number of thoughts arising out of my juvenile studies in theology; and I published it because, at a time when a young man's expectation of life was a rapidly dwindling asset, I wished at any rate to leave one philosophical publication behind me, and hated (as I still hate) leaving a decision of that kind to executors.

VI

THE DECAY OF REALISM

THE War ended, I came back to Oxford an opponent of the 'realists'. I had not yet learnt the uselessness of reading papers and holding discussions on philosophical subjects; so, with the intention of putting my cards on the table, I read a paper to my colleagues, trying to convince them that Cook Wilson's central positive doctrine, 'knowing makes no difference to what is known', was meaningless. I argued that any one who claimed, as Cook Wilson did, to be sure of this, was in effect claiming to know what he was simultaneously defining as unknown. For if you know that no difference is made to a thing θ by the presence or absence of a certain condition c, you know what θ is like with c, and also what θ is like without c, and on comparing the two find no difference. This involves knowing what θ is like without c; in the present case, knowing what you defined as the unknown.

My subject was not limited to that formula. I reviewed a number of logical doctrines expounded in Cook Wilson's lectures and pointed out that they were borrowed from Bradley; and I went so far as to say that, except for this one nonsensical phrase about knowledge making no difference to what is known, 'realism' had no positive doctrines of its own at all but had stolen all that it had from the school of thought which it was primarily concerned to discredit. And I described 'realism' in consequence as 'the undischarged bankrupt of modern philosophy'.

That description might have seemed less just some years later, when the 'realist' school could point to such assets as Alexander's *Space Time and Deity* and Whitehead's *Process and Reality*. But even those great works illustrate my point. Each of them is a system of *Naturphilosophie* as the term was understood by the post-Kantians. Alexander's philosophy of nature is even more closely modelled on the *Critique of Pure Reason* than was Hegel's; in many important ways it is very much like what that 'Metaphysics of Nature' would presumably have been which Kant promised but never wrote. In Whitehead the resemblance is more with Hegel; and the author, though he does not seem to be acquainted with Hegel, is not wholly unaware of this, for he describes the book as an attempt to do over again the work of 'idealism', 'but from a realist point of view'.

Actually, however, if 'realism' means the doctrine that the known is independent of, and unaffected by, the knowing it, Whitehead is not a 'realist' at all; for his 'philosophy of organism' commits him to the view that everything which forms an element in a given 'situation' is connected with everything else in that situation, not merely by a relation of compresence, but by interdependence. It follows that, where one element in a situation is a mind, and a second element something known to that mind, the knower and the known are interdependent. This is precisely the doctrine which it was the chief aim of the 'realists' to deny.

Alexander, whose British Academy paper on *The Essence of Realism*, one of the earliest and most important documents of the school, had made just that point, did not forget it in *Space Time and Deity*; nevertheless, the main body of that noble book consists of ideas borrowed from Kant and Hegel, to which a 'realistic' façade has been attached. It is none the worse for that. Whitehead's cosmology is constructed on an anti-'realistic' principle; Alexander's is built up of non-'realistic' materials. Neither can be used as evidence that modern English 'realism' is fertile in cosmological ideas; it would be more plausible to use them as evidence that English philosophy, at any rate in the persons of two very fine philosophers, is beginning to recover from the blight of 'realism' and re-establishing contact with the tradition which 'realism' meant to break.

Different people will differ as to whether a given state of things is a blight or not. The tailless fox preached taillessness. I have already said of 'realism' that its positive doctrine was nugatory, its critical technique deadly: all the deadlier because its effectiveness did not depend on errors native to the doctrines criticized, but on a kind of disintegration produced by itself in whatever it touched. It was therefore inevitable that by degrees 'realism' should part with all positive doctrines whatever, congratulating itself at each new jettison that it was rid of a knave.

Among the first of these consequences was the attack on moral philosophy. Moral philosophy, from the days of Socrates down to our own lifetime, had been regarded as an attempt to think out more clearly the issues involved in conduct, for the sake of acting better. In 1912 Prichard announced that moral philosophy as so understood was based on a mistake, and advocated a new kind of moral philosophy, purely theoretical, in which the workings of the moral consciousness should be scientifically studied as if they were the movements of the planets, and no attempt made to interfere with them. And Bertrand Russell at Cambridge proposed in the same spirit, and on grounds whose difference was only superficial, the extrusion of ethics from the body of philosophy.

The 'realist' philosophers who adopted this new programme were all, or nearly all, teachers of young men and young women. Their pupils, with habits and characters yet unformed, stood on the threshold of life; many of them on the threshold of public life. Half a century earlier, young people in that position had been told that by thinking about what they were doing, or were about to do, they would become likely on the whole to do it better; and that some understanding of the nature of moral or political action, some attempt to formulate ideals and principles, was an indispensable condition of engaging creditably in these activities themselves. And their teachers, when introducing them to the study of moral and political theory, would say to them, whether in words or not— the most important things that one says are often not said in words—'Take this subject seriously, because whether you understand it or not will make a difference to your whole lives'. The 'realist', on the contrary, said to his pupils, 'If it interests you to study this, do so; but don't think it will be of any use to you. Remember the great principle of realism, that nothing is affected by being known. That is as true of human action as of anything else. Moral philosophy is only the theory of moral action: it can't therefore make any difference to the practice of moral action. People can act just as morally without it as with it. I stand here as a moral philosopher; I will try to tell you what acting morally is, but don't expect me to tell you how to do it.'

At the moment, I am not concerned with the sophisms underlying this programme, but with its consequences. The pupils, whether or not they expected a philosophy that should give them, as that of Green's school had given their fathers, ideals to live for and principles to live by, did not get it; and were told that no philosopher (except of course a bogus philosopher) would even try to give it. The inference which any pupil could draw for himself was that for guidance in the problems of life, since one must not seek it from thinkers or from thinking, from ideals or from principles, one must look to people who were not thinkers (but fools), to processes that were not thinking (but passion), to aims that were not ideals (but caprices), and to rules that were not principles (but rules of expediency). If the realists had wanted to train up a generation of Englishmen and Englishwomen expressly as the potential dupes of every adventurer in morals or politics, commerce or religion, who should appeal to their emotions and promise them private gains which he neither could procure them nor even meant to procure them, no better way of doing it could have been discovered.

The result of all this might have been even worse than it has been, but for the fact that the 'realists' discredited themselves with their pupils before their lessons could take effect. This self-stultification was a gradual and piecemeal business. Not only did they jettison the entire body of traditional ethics; as soon as they began work on their new brand of moral theory, whatever doctrine concerning moral action was tested, to show whether it was fit to form part of that theory, was found wanting. Another traditional philosophical science which was thrown bodily overboard was the theory of knowledge; for although 'realism' began by defining itself as a theory of knowledge pure and simple, its votaries before long discovered that a theory of knowledge was a contradiction in terms. Another was political theory; this they destroyed by denying the conception of a 'common good', the fundamental idea of all social life, and insisting that all 'goods' were private. In this process, by which anything that could be recognized as a philosophical doctrine was stuck up and shot to pieces by the 'realistic' criticism, the 'realists' little by little destroyed everything in the way of positive doctrine that they had ever possessed. Once more, I am concerned only with the effect on their pupils. It was (how could it not have been?) to convince them that philosophy was a silly and trifling game, and to give them a lifelong contempt for the subject and a lifelong grudge against the men who had wasted their time by forcing it upon their attention.

That this did actually happen any one could see. The school of Green had taught that philosophy was not a preserve for professional philosophers, but every one's business; and the pupils of this school had gradually formed a block of opinion in the country whose members, though not professional philosophers, were interested in the subject, regarded it as important, and did not feel themselves debarred by their amateur status from expressing their own opinions about it. As these men died, no one took their place; and by about 1920 I found myself asking, 'Why is it that nowadays no Oxford man, unless he is either about 70 years old or else a teacher of philosophy at Oxford or elsewhere, regards philosophy as anything but a futile parlour game?' The answer was not difficult to find, and was confirmed by the fact that the 'realists', unlike the school of Green, did think philosophy a preserve for professional philosophers, and were loud in their contempt of philosophical utterances by historians, natural scientists, theologians, and other amateurs.

The fox was tailless, and knew it. But this mental kind of decaudation, when people part with their morals, their religion, the learning they acquired at school, and so forth, is commonly regarded by the tailless as an improvement in their condition; and so it was with the 'realists'. They were glad to have eradicated from the philosophical schools that confusion of philosophy with pulpit oratory which was involved in the bad old theory that moral philosophy is taught with a view to making the pupils better men. They were proud to have excogitated a philosophy so pure from the sordid taint of utility that they could lay their hands on their hearts and say it was no use at all; a philosophy so scientific that no one whose life was not a life of pure research could appreciate it, and so abstruse that only a whole-time student, and a very clever man at that, could understand it. They were quite resigned to the contempt of fools and amateurs. If anybody differed from them on these points, it could only be because his intellect was weak or his motives bad.

The latter end of the 'realist' movement is one of those things whose history will never be written. It is a story of how the men who best understood the ideas of the original 'realists', and tried hardest to remain loyal to them, found one piece of ground after another slipping from under their feet, and stumbled from one temporary and patchwork philosophy to another in a kind of intellectual nightmare. One of them, Bertrand Russell, a gifted and accomplished writer, has left records of his successive attempts at a philosophy; but most of them are, or were, less articulate, or else struck dumb by their sufferings; and when they and their friends are dead no one will ever know how their lives were spent. What I myself know about it I shall certainly not repeat.

But if the 'realism' of my youth is dead, it has left not only a heritage of general prejudice against philosophy as such, but a partial heir. Its propositional logic, as worked out by Bertrand Russell and A. N. Whitehead, has inspired a school of thought which is continuing the good work of jettisoning whatever can be recognized as positive doctrine by reviving the old positivist attack on metaphysics. After what I have said about propositional logic, I need not pause to explain why I think that this school, with all its ingenuity and pertinacity, is only building card-houses out of a pack of lies. But I do not think that altogether a waste of time. The 'idealistic' logic, to which this school is related as Oxford 'realism' was related to the school of Green, was a confused mixture of truth and error. Mostly it was a propositional logic; but in part it was a logic of question and answer. I would rather its successors had chosen to eradicate the error and develop the truth; but they have decided to do the opposite, and I am not ungrateful. In logic I am a revolutionary; and like other revolutionaries I can thank God for the reactionaries. They clarify the issue.

VII

THE HISTORY OF PHILOSOPHY

So far as my philosophical ideas were concerned, I was now cut off not only from the 'realist' school to which most of my colleagues belonged, but from every other school of thought in England, I might almost say in the world. This did not imply social isolation. I enjoyed, in both senses of that word, the friendship and society of a great many philosophers, in Oxford and at other places in the British Isles and indeed elsewhere. I also enjoyed their philosophical conversation and liked to hear, and engage in, their discussions.

These went on with unfailing regularity. I used to meet a dozen or so of my colleagues every week in order to discuss a topic or a view propounded by one of us, and more ceremoniously a body called the Oxford Philosophical Society met on Sunday evenings two or three times a term for the reading and discussion of a paper. Once a year the thing became a debauch, in the annual joint meeting in some university town of various philosophical societies at which papers and discussions went on for days together. Such gatherings introduced one to people in one's own profession, and they were useful as showing how delightful might be the society of men whose doctrines one disapproved, or how unnecessary it was to waste time over the works of some much advertised person who had only to stand up and speak in order to proclaim himself an impostor. But these discussions serve no philosophical purpose. *Viva voce* philosophy is an excellent thing as between tutor and pupil; it may be valuable as between two intimate friends; it is tolerable as between a few friends who know each other very well; but in all these cases its only value is to make one party acquainted with the views of the other. Where it becomes argument, directed to refutation and conviction, it is useless, for (in my long experience, at least) no one has ever been convinced by it. Where it becomes general discussion it is an outrage. One of the company reads a paper, and the rest discuss it with a fluency directly proportional to their ignorance. To shine on such occasions one should have a rather obtuse, insensitive mind and a ready tongue. Whatever may be true of parrots, philosophers who cannot talk probably think the more, and those who think a lot certainly talk the less.

It was not so very unfortunate, therefore, that when I took part in these weekly arguments the problems had always to be other people's problems and the methods of handling them other people's methods; and that if I tried to raise the problems which I found especially interesting, or to conduct a discussion according to what I thought the right methods, I was met by a greater or less degree of incomprehension, or by the well-known symptoms of an outraged philosophical conscience. For these experiments very soon taught me what it was important for me to learn: that I must do my own work by myself, and not expect my colleagues in the philosophical profession to give me any help.

But this did not mean that I ceased to take part in their discussions. In another chapter I have explained that, according to my own 'logic of question and answer', a philosopher's doctrines are his answers to certain questions he has asked himself, and no one who does not understand what the questions are can hope to understand the doctrines. The same logic committed me to the view that any one can understand any philosopher's doctrines if he can grasp the questions which they are intended to answer. Those questions need not be his own; they may belong to a thought-complex very different from any that is spontaneously going on in his own mind; but this ought not to prevent him from understanding them and judging whether the persons interested in them are answering them rightly or wrongly.

This view makes it a point of honour for any philosopher holding it to take part in the discussion of problems that are not his own problems, and to help in the working-out of philosophies that are not his own philosophy. Hence, when other philosophers discussed problems arising out of distinctions I thought false, or based on principles I thought unsound, I would enter into the discussion in precisely the same spirit in which I would enter into some ancient philosophical controversy, not expecting the disputants to be interested in my problems, but very definitely requiring of myself an interest in theirs.

It was perhaps as well for me that I did not expect

other philosophers to understand me. At that time, any one opposing the 'realists' was automatically classified as an 'idealist', which meant a belated survivor of Green's school. There was no ready-made class into which you could put a philosopher who, after a thorough training in 'realism', had revolted against it and arrived at conclusions of his own quite unlike anything the school of Green had taught. So, in spite of occasional remonstrances, that was how I found myself classified. I became used to it; otherwise I might have been too much annoyed to keep that rule against answering critics which every one must keep who has work of his own to do, when one of the 'realists' (not an Oxford man), reviewing the first book in which I tried to indicate my position, dismissed it in a few lines as 'the usual idealistic nonsense'.

The book was *Speculum Mentis*, published in 1924. It is a bad book in many ways.[1] The position laid

[1] Since writing that sentence, I have read *Speculum Mentis* for the first time since it was published, and find it much better than I remembered. It is a record, not so very obscure in expression, of a good deal of genuine thinking. If much of it now fails to satisfy me, that is because I have gone on thinking since I wrote it, and therefore much of it needs to be supplemented and qualified. There is not a great deal that needs to be retracted.

About answering critics: I have never made, and shall never make, any public answer to any public criticism passed upon my work. I value my time too highly. Now and then I have thought it civil to comment briefly, in a private letter, on criticisms made by letter or on printed criticisms of which the author has sent me a copy. Such comments, of course, are not replies, and in no circumstances should I authorize their publication.

down in it was incompletely thought out and unskil-
fully expressed; and for most readers concealed, rather
than illustrated, by a dense incrustation of miscel-
laneous detail. I should entirely sympathize with a
reviewer who had said he could make neither head
nor tail of it, or had described it as nonsense. But
any one who had been intelligent enough to see what
I was trying to say would have realized, had he not
been grossly ignorant, that it was neither 'usual' nor
'idealistic'.

To return. This habit of following and taking part
in discussions where both subject and method were
other people's proved extremely valuable to me. I
found it not only a delightful task, but a magnificent
exercise, to follow the work of contemporary philosophers whose views differed widely from my own, to
write essays developing their positions and applying
them to topics they had not dealt with, to reconstruct
their problems in my own mind, and to study, often
with the liveliest admiration, the way in which they
had tried to solve them. This power of enjoying and
admiring the work of other philosophers, no matter
how widely their philosophies differed from mine,
was not always pleasing to my colleagues. Some of
them it perhaps deceived into thinking I had no
serious convictions of my own; others it annoyed, as
a cowardly refusal to defend whatever convictions I
had. 'I wish you'd get off the fence,' said Prichard to
me once, in a voice of the liveliest exasperation, at
one of our weekly discussions, when two rival theories
were being canvassed (I forget what they were) both

of which I regarded as based on one and the same mistake. Twenty years' familiarity with his mind had taught me that it was no use trying to explain. If I had begun, he would have broken in, and in five minutes refuted *secundum artem* everything he thought I was going to say.

This way of treating other people's thoughts, though formally deducible from my 'logic of question and answer', had been my habit long before I began working that logic out. To think in that way about philosophies not your own, as I have hinted, is to think about them historically. I dare say I was not more than six or seven when I first saw that the only way to tackle any historical question, such as the tactics of Trafalgar—I mention Trafalgar, because naval history was a childish passion of mine, and Trafalgar my pet battle—was to see what the different people concerned were trying to do. History did not mean knowing what events followed what. It meant getting inside other people's heads, looking at their situation through their eyes, and thinking for yourself whether the way in which they tackled it was the right way. Unless you can see the battle through the eyes of a man brought up in sailing-ships armed with broadsides of short-range muzzle-loading guns, you are not even a beginner in naval history, you are right outside it. If you allow yourself to think for a moment about the tactics of Trafalgar as if the ships were driven by steam and armed with long-range breech-loading guns, you have for that moment allowed yourself to drift outside the region of history altogether.

It was a doctrine of 'realism' (and this is why Prichard was so cross with me) that in this sense of the word history there is no history of philosophy. The 'realists' thought that the problems with which philosophy is concerned were unchanging. They thought that Plato, Aristotle, the Epicureans, the Stoics, the Schoolmen, the Cartesians, &c., had all asked themselves the same set of questions, and had given different answers to them. For example, they thought that the same problems which are discussed in modern ethical theory were discussed in Plato's *Republic* and Aristotle's *Ethics*; and that it was a man's work to ask himself whether Aristotle or Kant was right on the points over which they differ concerning the nature of duty.

In a quite different sense of the word, the 'realists' certainly thought that philosophy has a history. The different answers which various philosophers have given to the eternal questions of philosophy have been given, of course, in a certain order and at various dates; and the 'history' of philosophy is the study by which people ascertain what answers have been given to these questions, in what order, and at what dates. In that sense, the question, 'what was Aristotle's theory of duty?' would be an 'historical' question. And it would be wholly separate from the philosophical question, 'was it true?' Thus the 'history' of philosophy was an inquiry which had nothing to do with the question whether Plato's theory of Ideas (for example) was true or false, but only with the question what it was.

The Oxford tradition insisted upon a fine training in philosophical scholarship, the knowledge of some at least among the classical works of philosophical literature and the ability to interpret them. Under the reign of 'realism' this tradition certainly survived, and was in fact the most valuable part of an Oxford philosophical training; but it weakened almost year by year. Successive boards of examiners in 'Greats' used to complain that the standard of work on Greek philosophy was declining. When I myself examined in the middle 1920's, I found that very few candidates showed any first-hand knowledge of any authors about whom they wrote. What they knew was their notes of the lectures they had attended upon these authors, and the lecturers' criticisms of their philosophies. This decline of interest in philosophical history was openly encouraged by the 'realists'; it was one of their most respected leaders who, expressly on the ground that the 'history' of philosophy was a subject without philosophical interest, procured the abolition of the paper so entitled in the school of Philosophy, Politics, and Economics.

During the War, in the course of my meditations on the Albert Memorial, I set myself to reconsider this 'realist' attitude towards the history of philosophy. Was it really true, I asked myself, that the problems of philosophy were, even in the loosest sense of that word, eternal? Was it really true that different philosophies were different attempts to answer the same questions? I soon discovered that it was not true; it was merely a vulgar error, consequent on a kind of historical myopia which, deceived by superficial resemblances, failed to detect profound differences.

The first point at which I saw a perfectly clear gleam of daylight was in political theory. Take Plato's *Republic* and Hobbes's *Leviathan*, so far as they are concerned with politics. Obviously the political theories they set forth are not the same. But do they represent two different theories of the same thing? Can you say that the *Republic* gives one account of 'the nature of the State' and the *Leviathan* another? No; because Plato's 'State' is the Greek πόλις, and Hobbes's is the absolutist State of the seventeenth century. The 'realist' answer is easy: certainly Plato's State is different from Hobbes's, but they are both States; so the theories are theories of the State. Indeed, what did you mean by calling them both political, if not that they were theories of the same thing?

It was obvious to me that this was only a piece of logical bluff, and that if instead of logic-chopping you got down to brass tacks and called for definitions of the 'State' as Plato conceived it and as Hobbes conceived it, you would find that the differences between them were not superficial but went down to essentials. You can call the two things the same if you insist; but if you do, you must admit that the thing has got *diablement changé en route*, so that the 'nature of the State' in Plato's time was genuinely different from the 'nature of the State' in Hobbes's. I do not mean the empirical nature of the State; I mean the ideal nature of the State. What even the best and wisest of those who are engaged in politics are trying to do has altered.

Plato's *Republic* is an attempt at a theory of one thing; Hobbes's *Leviathan* an attempt at a theory of something else.

There is, of course, a connexion between these two things; but it is not the kind of connexion that the 'realists' thought it was. Anybody would admit that Plato's *Republic* and Hobbes's *Leviathan* are about two things which are in one way the same thing and in another way different. That is not in dispute. What is in dispute is the kind of sameness and the kind of difference. The 'realists' thought that the sameness was the sameness of a 'universal', and the difference the difference between two instances of that universal. But this is not so. The sameness is the sameness of an historical process, and the difference is the difference between one thing which in the course of that process has turned into something else, and the other thing into which it has turned. Plato's πόλις and Hobbes's absolutist State are related by a traceable historical process, whereby one has turned into the other; any one who ignores that process, denies the difference between them, and argues that where Plato's political theory contradicts Hobbes's one of them must be wrong, is saying the thing that is not.

Pursuing this line of inquiry, I soon realized that the history of political theory is not the history of different answers given to one and the same question, but the history of a problem more or less constantly changing, whose solution was changing with it. The 'form of the πόλις' is not, as Plato seems to have thought, the one and only ideal of human society possible to intelligent men. It is not something eternally laid up in heaven and eternally envisaged, as the goal of their efforts, by all good statesmen of whatever age and country. It was the ideal of human society as that ideal was conceived by the Greeks of Plato's own time. By the time of Hobbes, people had changed their minds not only about what was possible in the way of social organization, but about what was desirable. Their ideals were different. And consequently the political philosophers whose business it was to give a reasoned statement of these ideals had a different task before them; one which, if it was to be rightly discharged, must be discharged differently.

The clue, once found, was easily applied elsewhere. It was not difficult to see that, just as the Greek πόλις could not be legitimately translated by the modern word 'State', except with a warning that the two things are in various essential ways different, and a statement of what these differences are; so, in ethics, a Greek word like δεῖ cannot be legitimately translated by using the word 'ought', if that word carries with it the notion of what is sometimes called 'moral obligation'. Was there any Greek word or phrase to express that notion? The 'realists' said there was; but they stultified themselves by adding that the 'theories of moral obligation' expounded by Greek writers differed from modern theories such as Kant's about the same thing. How did they know that the Greek and the Kantian theories were about the same thing? Oh, because δεῖ (or whatever word it was) is the Greek for 'ought'.

It was like having a nightmare about a man who had got it into his head that τριήρης was the Greek for 'steamer', and when it was pointed out to him that descriptions of triremes in Greek writers were at any rate not very good descriptions of steamers, replied triumphantly, 'That is just what I say. These Greek philosophers' (or, 'these modern philosophers', according to which side he was on in the good old controversy between the Ancients and the Moderns) 'were terribly muddle-headed, and their theory of steamers is all wrong'. If you tried to explain that τριήρης does not mean steamer at all but something different, he would reply, 'Then what does it mean?' and in ten minutes he would show you that you didn't know; you couldn't draw a trireme, or make a model of one, or even describe exactly how it worked. And having annihilated you, he would go on for the rest of his life translating τριήρης 'steamer'.

If he had not been quite so clever, he might have known that by a careful sifting and interpretation of the evidence you can arrive at some conclusions, though certainly incomplete ones, about what a trireme was like. And by similar treatment of the evidence you can arrive at some conclusions about the meaning of words like δεῖ. But in both cases you have to approach the matter from an historical point of view, not from that of a minute philosopher; and in the conviction that whatever the Greek word in question means it will not necessarily (indeed, not probably) mean anything that can be rendered by one word, if indeed by any words, in English.

Ideals of personal conduct are just as impermanent as ideals of social organization. Not only that, but what is meant by calling them ideals is subject to the same change. The 'realists' knew that different peoples, and the same peoples at different times, held different views, and were quite entitled to hold different views, about how a man ought to behave; but they thought that the phrase 'ought to behave' had a meaning which was one, unchanging, and eternal. They were wrong. The literature of European moral philosophy, from the Greeks onwards, was in their hands and on their shelves to tell them so; but they evaded the lesson by systematically mistranslating the passages from which they might have learnt it.

In metaphysics the corresponding analysis was easy to one who had been addicted from childhood to the history of science. I could not but see, for example, when Einstein set philosophers talking about relativity, that philosophers' convictions about the eternity of problems or conceptions were as baseless as a young girl's conviction that this year's hats are the only ones that could ever have been worn by a sane woman. One heard them maintaining the 'axiomatic' or 'self-evident' character of doctrines about matter, motion, and so forth which had first been propounded by very adventurous thinkers, at risk of their own liberty and life, three or four hundred years ago, and had become part of every educated European's beliefs only after long and fanatical propaganda in the eighteenth century.

It became clear to me that metaphysics (as its very

name might show, though people still use the word as if it had been 'paraphysics') is no futile attempt at knowing what lies beyond the limits of experience, but is primarily at any given time an attempt to discover what the people of that time believe about the world's general nature; such beliefs being the presuppositions of all their 'physics', that is, their inquiries into its detail. Secondarily, it is the attempt to discover the corresponding presuppositions of other peoples and other times, and to follow the historical process by which one set of presuppositions has turned into another.

The question what presuppositions underlie the 'physics' or natural science of a certain people at a certain time is as purely historical a question as what kind of clothes they wear. And this is the question that metaphysicians have to answer. It is not their business to raise the further question whether, among the various beliefs on this subject that various peoples hold and have held, this one or that one is true. This question, when raised, would always be found, as it always has been found, unanswerable; and if there is anything in my 'logic of question and answer' that is not to be wondered at, for the beliefs whose history the metaphysician has to study are not answers to questions but only presuppositions of questions, and therefore the distinction between what is true and what is false does not apply to them, but only the distinction between what is presupposed and what is not presupposed. A presupposition of one question may be the answer to another question. The beliefs which a metaphysician tries to study and codify are presuppositions of the questions asked by natural scientists, but are not answers to any questions at all. This might be expressed by calling them 'absolute' presuppositions.

But the statements which any competent metaphysician tries to make or refute, substantiate or undermine, are themselves certainly true or false; for they are answers to questions about the history of these presuppositions. This was my answer to the rather threadbare question 'how can metaphysics become a science?' If science means a naturalistic science, the answer is that it had better not try. If science means an organized body of knowledge, the answer is: by becoming what it always has been; that is, frankly claiming its proper status as an historical inquiry in which, on the one hand, the beliefs of a given set of people at a given time concerning the nature of the world are exhibited as a single complex of contemporaneous fact, like, say, the British constitution as it stands to-day; and, on the other hand, the origin of these beliefs is inquired into, and it is found that during a certain space of time they have come into existence by certain changes out of certain others.

By degrees I found that there was no recognized branch of philosophy to which the principle did not apply that its problems, as well as the solutions proposed for them, had their own history. The conception of 'eternal problems' disappeared entirely, except so far as any historical fact could be called eternal because it had happened once for all, and accordingly any problem could be called eternal because it had arisen once for all and once for all been solved.[1] I found (and it required a good deal of hard detailed work in the history of thought) that most of the conceptions round which revolve the controversies of modern philosophy, conceptions designated by words like 'state', 'ought', 'matter', 'cause', had appeared on the horizon of human thought at ascertainable times in the past, often not very distant times, and that the philosophical controversies of other ages had revolved round other conceptions, not indeed unrelated to ours, but not, except by a person quite blind to historical truth, indistinguishable from them.

Having thus with regard to the supposed permanence of philosophical problems found the 'realist' conception of philosophical history false at every point where I could think of testing it, I turned to another aspect of the same conception: namely the 'realists'' distinction between the 'historical' question 'what was So-and-so's theory on such and such a matter?' and the 'philosophical' question 'was he right?'

This distinction was soon condemned as fallacious. I will not here explain, since the reader can easily see it for himself, how it broke down in the light of the

[1] If 'eternal' is used in its vulgar and inaccurate sense, as equivalent to 'lasting for a considerable time', the phrase 'eternal problem' may be used to designate collectively a series of problems connected by a process of historical change, such that their continuity is discernible even by the presumably rather unintelligent eye of the person who thus misuses the word, but the differences between them not so discernible.

question 'how is the so-called philosophical issue to
be settled?' and the answer that it could only be settled
by what I was simultaneously discovering to be the
sophistical methods of 'realist' criticism. I will rather
point out that the alleged distinction between the
historical question and the philosophical must be
false, because it presupposes the permanence of philosophical problems. If there were a permanent problem P, we could ask 'what did Kant, or Leibniz, or
Berkeley, think about P?' and if that question could
be answered, we could then go on to ask 'was Kant, or
Leibniz, or Berkeley, right in what he thought about
P?' But what is thought to be a permanent problem P
is really a number of transitory problems $p_1\ p_2\ p_3 \ldots$
whose individual peculiarities are blurred by the historical myopia of the person who lumps them together
under the one name P. It follows that we cannot fish
the problem P out of the hyperuranian lucky-bag, hold
it up, and say 'what did So-and-so think about this?'
We have to begin, as poor devils of historians begin,
from the other end. We have to study documents and
interpret them. We have to say 'here is a passage of
Leibniz; what is it about? what is the problem with
which it deals?' Perhaps we label that problem p_{14}.
Then comes the question 'Does Leibniz here deal
with p_{14} rightly or wrongly?' The answer to this is not
quite so simple as the 'realists' think. If Leibniz when
he wrote this passage was so confused in his mind as
to make a complete mess of the job of solving his problem, he was bound at the same time to mix up his own
tracks so completely that no reader could see quite

clearly what his problem had been. For one and the same passage states his solution and serves as evidence of what the problem was. The fact that we can identify his problem is proof that he has solved it; for we only know what the problem was by arguing back from the solution.

If anybody chooses to deny this, I will not try to convince him. Everybody who has learnt to think historically knows it already; and no amount of argument could teach it to a person who had not learnt to think historically. How can we discover what the tactical problem was that Nelson set himself at Trafalgar? Only by studying the tactics he pursued in the battle. We argue back from the solution to the problem. What else could we do? Even if we had the original typescript of the coded orders issued by wireless to his captains a few hours before the battle began, this would not tell us that he had not changed his mind at the last moment, extemporized a new plan on seeing some new factor in the situation, and trusted his captains to understand what he was doing and to back him up. Naval historians think it worth while to argue about Nelson's tactical plan at Trafalgar because he won the battle. It is not worth while arguing about Villeneuve's plan. He did not succeed in carrying it out, and therefore no one will ever know what it was. We can only guess. And guessing is not history.

A teacher who puts into his pupils' hands a philosophical text, and invites them to attend to a certain passage, may therefore say to them, 'This is a confused passage; we can see that the author was thinking about

some problem or other, and we may reasonably con-
jecture that it was a problem somewhat like that discussed in such and such a passage by So-and-so. But
he is muddled about the business, and no one can ever
tell exactly what it was that worried the poor man.'
He may say this; but if he does, his pupils will not
greatly cherish his memory in after life. He had no
business to waste their time on a passage of that sort.

Or, pointing them to a different passage, he may say,
'here our author, being neither illiterate nor idiotic
(which is why I am asking you to study his works), has
expressed in such a way that we can understand it a
thought that was worth expressing. At first sight you
cannot tell what he is trying to say. But if you will
think carefully about the passage you will see that he
is answering a question which he has taken the trouble
to formulate in his mind with great precision. What
you are reading is his answer. Now tell me what the
question was.'

But he cannot have it both ways. He cannot say
'our author is here trying to answer the following question. . . . That is a question which all philosophers ask
themselves sooner or later; the right answer to it, as
given by Plato or Kant or Wittgenstein, is. . . . Our
author is giving one of the wrong answers. The refutation of his erroneous view is as follows.' His claim to
know what question the author is asking is a fraud
which any one could expose by asking for his evidence.
As a matter of fact, he is not basing his assertion on
evidence; he is only trotting out some philosophical
question of which the passage vaguely reminds him.

For me, then, there were not two separate sets of questions to be asked, one historical and one philosophical, about a given passage in a given philosophical author. There was one set only, historical. The study of Plato was, in my eyes, of the same kind as the study of Thucydides. The study of Greek philosophy and the study of Greek warfare are both historical studies. But this did not mean that the question 'was Plato right to think as he did on such and such a question?' was to be left unanswered. As well suggest that the question 'was Phormio right to row round the Corinthians' circle?' must be left unanswered because it goes outside the province of naval history, whose only concern with Phormio is to find out what he did. What lunatic idea of history is this, which would imply that it is history that Phormio rowed round the Corinthians, but not that he beat the Corinthians by doing it? Are we haunted by the ghost of Ranke, gibbering something about 'what exactly happened', and has this frightened us into forgetting that victories, as well as tactical manœuvres, are things that happen, or at any rate things that did happen before modern progress abolished them?

These ideas, except such part of them as I had already worked out before returning to Oxford, became clear to me soon afterwards. It would have been quite useless to put them before my colleagues. The 'realists', whose critical technique was flawless and whose mastery of it was perfect, would have demolished them in no time. That would not have made me give them up; for I had already analysed the principles of 'realist' criticism and knew that what it so admirably demolished was not (or not necessarily) the views it ostensibly attacked, but the critic's own perversion of these views; although the 'realist' could never distinguish between the perversion and the reality, because the perversion was simply the reality as seen through his distorting spectacles. If I had stated these ideas to the leaders of the 'realist' school, they would have said, as I have heard them say a hundred times, 'you don't mean that; what you mean is . . .' and then would have followed a caricature of my ideas in terms of 'realist' principles, with sandbags for arms and legs; all so beautifully done that I could hardly have restrained my impulse to cheer.

My job, after all, was not with my colleagues but with my pupils. According to the very ancient Oxford tradition—a tradition far older than Oxford itself—philosophy is taught by reading, expounding, and commenting on philosophical texts. Because the tradition is a living one, these texts are not those of ancient authors alone. The repertory of texts, which is nowhere printed and has no statutory sanction, is constantly changing; though it does not change very fast, and rightly, since no book is ripe for use in this peculiar way until it has become a classic. Yesterday's work of genius may have revolutionized its subject; but, even so, the best way of teaching undergraduates exactly how the subject has been revolutionized is by lecturing on the old classics and showing in your commentary how their doctrine has been modified.

Here was a field of activity which exactly suited me.

My inclinations have always led me rather towards detail than towards generalization; a general principle never comes to life in my mind except by exhibiting itself in its various special forms and in crowds of instances for each form. I did not really feel any great desire to expound the philosophical ideas I have been setting forth in these chapters, whether to my colleagues or to the public. As I have said, I tried to expound them; but when *Truth and Contradiction* was rejected by a publisher and my attack on 'realist' principles ignored by my colleagues, I felt justified in turning to the far more congenial task of applying them and thus testing them empirically. This I could now do, for several hours daily, by teaching my pupils to obey certain rules in their study of philosophical texts.

In an earlier chapter I have stated the first rule which I impressed upon my pupils, 'never accept criticism of any author before satisfying yourself of its relevance'. By now meditation on the Albert Memorial had taught me a second, namely, 'reconstruct the problem'; or, 'never think you understand any statement made by a philosopher until you have decided, with the utmost possible accuracy, what the question is to which he means it for an answer'.

These rules were never formulated in so many words. But they were exemplified by constant practice. From my return to Oxford until my becoming a professor, almost my whole teaching life as a Fellow of Pembroke College was spent in showing pupils how to read a philosophical text. It certainly interested the pupils. An undergraduate who had been merely re-pelled by ready-made refutations of a doctrine would grow excited when his tutor said, 'Let us see, first, that you really know what the man says, and what the question is that he is trying to answer', and books would be brought out and read and explained, and the rest of the hour would pass in a flash. And for myself it was no less salutary. Over and over again, I would return to a familiar passage whose meaning I thought I knew—had it not been expounded by numerous learned commentators, and were they not more or less agreed about it?—to find that, under this fresh scrutiny, the old interpretation melted away and some quite different meaning began to take form. Thus the history of philosophy, which my 'realist' friends thought a subject without philosophical sig-nificance, became for me a source of unfailing, and strictly philosophical, interest and delight; and for my pupils, I dare to hope, neither uninstructive nor unamusing.

But, of course, it was no longer a 'closed' subject. It was no longer a body of facts which a very, very learned man might know, or a very, very big book enumerate, in their completeness. It was an 'open' subject, an inexhaustible fountain of problems, old problems re-opened and new problems formulated that had not been formulated until now. Above all, it was a constant warfare against the dogmas, often posi-tively erroneous, and always vicious in so far as they were dogmatic, of that putrefying corpse of historical thought, the 'information' to be found in text-books.

For in the history of philosophy, as in every other kind, nothing capable of being learnt by heart, nothing capable of being memorized, is history.

And if anybody had objected that in what I call 'open' history one couldn't see the wood for the trees, I should have answered, who wants to? A tree is a thing to look at; but a wood is not a thing to look at, it is a thing to live in.

VIII

THE NEED FOR A PHILOSOPHY OF HISTORY

My life's work hitherto, as seen from my fiftieth year, has been in the main an attempt to bring about a *rapprochement* between philosophy and history. In the preceding chapter I have described one aspect of this *rapprochement*, namely my demand that when philosophers thought about the history of their own subject they should recognize that what they were thinking about was history, and should think about it in ways which did not disgrace the contemporary standards of historical thinking. From the first, however, I saw that more than this was involved. I was also demanding a philosophy of history.

This meant, in the first instance, a special branch of philosophical inquiry devoted to the special problems raised by historical thinking. Epistemological problems, such as one might group together under the question 'how is historical knowledge possible?' Metaphysical problems, concerned with the nature of the historian's subject-matter: the elucidation of terms like event, process, progress, civilization, and so forth. But this demand for a new branch of philosophy soon developed into the demand for a new kind of philosophy. I can best explain what I meant by analogy with the new kind of philosophy which grew up in the seventeenth century.

Soon after the beginning of that century, a number of intelligent people in western Europe began to see in a settled and steady manner what a few here and there had seen by fits and starts for the last hundred years or more: namely that the problems which ever since the time of early Greek philosophy had gone by the collective name of 'physics' were capable of being restated in a shape in which, with the double weapon of experiment and mathematics, one could now solve them. What was called Nature, they saw, had henceforth no secrets from man; only riddles which he had learnt the trick of answering. Or, more accurately, Nature was no longer a Sphinx asking man riddles; it was man that did the asking, and Nature, now, that he put to the torture until she gave him the answer to his questions.

This was an important event in human history. It was important enough to divide the philosophers of the period into two groups: those who understood its importance and those who did not. The first group comprised all those whose names are now generally known to students of philosophy. The second, an immensely greater host of good men, learned men, subtle men, sleep their long night unknown and unlamented, not because they did not find a poet to praise them; few philosophers do; but because they misread the signs of the times. They did not realize that the chief business of seventeenth-century philosophy was to reckon with seventeenth-century natural science; to solve the new problems that the new science had raised, and to envisage the old problems in the new forms which they had assumed, or would assume, when refracted into new shapes through the new scientific atmosphere.

The chief business of twentieth-century philosophy is to reckon with twentieth-century history. Until the late nineteenth and early twentieth centuries, historical studies had been in a condition analogous to that of natural science before Galileo.[1] In Galileo's time something happened to natural science (only a very ignorant or a very learned man would undertake to say briefly what it was) which suddenly and enormously increased the velocity of its progress and the width of its outlook. About the end of the nineteenth century something of the same kind was happening, more gradually and less spectacularly perhaps, but not less certainly, to history.

Until then, the writer of history had been in the last resort, however he might prune and pad, moralize and comment, a scissors-and-paste man. At bottom, his business was to know what 'the authorities' had said about the subject he was interested in, and to his authorities' statements he was tied by the leg, however long the rope and however flowery the turf over which it allowed him to circle. If his interest led him towards a subject on which there were no authori-

---

[1] Lord Acton in his Cambridge inaugural lecture in 1895 said very truly that historical studies had entered upon a new era in the second quarter of the nineteenth century. It would be an understatement to say that since 1800 history has passed through a Copernican revolution. Looking back from the present day one sees that a much greater revolution has been accomplished than that associated with the name of Copernicus.

ties, it led him into a desert where nothing was except the sands of ignorance and the mirage of imagination.

I will not pretend that my first visit to a modern excavation (it was my father's dig at the north tower of the Roman fort called Hardknot Castle; I was three weeks old, and they took me in a carpenter's bag) opened my eyes to the possibility of something different. But I grew up in a gradually thickening archaeological atmosphere; for my father, who as a professional painter was not very successful, turned more and more as he grew older to archaeology, for which he was brilliantly gifted; and at last, during school holidays, I learnt to distinguish the relics of ancient camps and cultivations from eskers and outcrops, was entrusted with the search for prehistoric remains in unexplored districts and the surveying of them when found, and spent two seasons working as his assistant in his now classical excavation of a Romano-British village.

This and similar experiences taught me that scissors and paste were not the only foundation of historical method. All you wanted, I could see, was a sufficiently extensive and sufficiently scientific development of such work, and it would teach you, not indeed everything, but a great deal, about subjects whose very existence must remain permanently unknown to historians who believed in authorities. I could see, too, that the same methods might be used to correct the authorities themselves, where they had been mistaken or untruthful. In either case, the idea of an historian as depending on what the authorities tell him was exploded.

All this might have been got from books ever since Boucher de Perthes began grubbing in gravel-pits; and long before it entered my head it had been familiar to the readers of newspapers. But I have never found it easy to learn anything from books, let alone newspapers. When I read my friends' articles about their excavations on the middle page of *The Times*, or the beautifully illustrated handbook that tells me how to look after a certain kind of motor, my brain seems to stop working. But give me half an hour on the excavation, with a student to show me what is what, or leave me alone with the motor and a box of tools, and things go better. So these ideas about history, however elementary and commonplace they might be, were at any rate solidly acquired. I had learnt by first-hand experience that history is not an affair of scissors and paste, but is much more like Bacon's notion of science. The historian has to decide exactly what it is that he wants to know; and if there is no authority to tell him, as in fact (one learns in time) there never is, he has to find a piece of land or something that has got the answer hidden in it, and get the answer out by fair means or foul.

That was as far as my philosophy of history had got when I went up to Oxford. There the revolution in historical method which had already attracted my notice was going busily and not silently forward. Sir Arthur Evans, early in the century, had begun to give a brilliant example of the new method by unearthing and reconstructing the long history of Bronze Age Knossos. The official reaction of Oxford was to cut out of Greek history (that is, from Greek history as a subject to be taught and examined in) everything down to the first Olympiad. Next, archaeology began to invade ancient history at the other end of its time-scale. Mommsen had shown how by statistical and other treatment of inscriptions the historian of the Roman Empire could answer questions that no one had dreamed of asking. Dragendorff had classified the shapes of 'Samian' pottery, and he and others had begun to date them. It was a recently established and exciting fact that by excavation you could recon-struct the history of Roman sites not mentioned in any authority and of events in Roman history not mentioned in any book. Owing to the work of Haver-field, whose interest embraced every branch and twig of Roman archaeology, and whose skill and learning as an epigraphist were comparable, we believed, only with those of Mommsen himself, these notions had taken a firm root in Oxford and were completely transforming the study of the Roman Empire.

To the inquiring mind of youth it made a piquant contrast that Greek historical studies, in those days, were still strictly scissors-and-paste. Greek archaeo-logy existed; had we not Percy Gardner? but it only served to adorn the tale told by the authorities, except when some bold revolutionary like D. G. Hogarth hinted that it might here and there fill in a gap. But, according to the orthodox view, the last event that had happened in Greek historical studies had been the discovery of Aristotle's *Constitution of Athens*; and the kind of thing that the undergraduate was supposed to do was to compare the two accounts of the Athenian Revolution given by Thucydides and Aristotle, and decide point by point which was the likelier to be right. And the great lecturer of the day on Greek history, E. M. Walker, was elaborately polite to archaeology in the way which only Pope has described, but lesser men can quite well understand, and weep if Atticus were he.

So Greek history was left high and dry by the tide of new methods; and for many years after this, until what I hope will be long remembered as the archonship of Alan Blakeway, it was notorious that able young men at Oxford, when devoting their lives to ancient history, specialized almost unanimously in the Roman Empire and left Greece to the scissors-and-paste men.

Haverfield himself, least philosophical of historians, cared nothing about the principles or the potentialities of the revolution he was leading. He never even seemed aware that a revolution was going on. He once complained to me that examiners in 'Greats' seemed bent on ignoring his lectures in the papers they set, and that in a general way his colleagues did not share his own attitude to history; but I do not think it occurred to him that there might be a reason for this neglect, or that differences between different historians' attitudes towards history might be worth reflecting upon.

As for the philosophers, their books and lectures

and conversations never once conveyed to me the smallest hint that any of them knew what was happening. They had inherited a tradition, dating back to the early seventeenth century, according to which the methods of natural science received the most painstaking scrutiny. It would have been considered a mark of gross ignorance in any of them not to have known something, indeed more than a mere something, about 'scientific' method, the part played in it by observation and reasoning respectively, the problems of induction, and so forth. Any of them, without special preparation, could have given an entire set of lectures on the problems of 'scientific' method. And when they discussed the theory of knowledge it was plain that, as a rule, they regarded the word 'knowledge' in that phrase as more or less equivalent to knowledge of the world of nature or physical world.

Their total neglect of history, as an example of knowledge, was to my mind all the odder because, whereas hardly any of them had ever been trained in natural science, practically all (I speak of Oxford philosophers) had read 'Greats' and therefore had undergone a course of advanced study in ancient history. Yet, in the whole literature of the 'realist' school at that time, I recollect only one passage which might even be mistaken for a treatment of history: the chapter in Joseph's *Logic* on 'The Historical Method'. When you turn it up, you find that the 'Historical Method' has nothing to do with history, but is a method used in natural science.

To say the very least of it, this gap was a discredit to

English philosophy. My 'realist' friends, when I said this to them, replied that there was no gap at all; that their theory of knowledge was a theory of knowledge, not a theory of this kind of knowledge or that kind of knowledge; that certainly it applied to 'scientific' knowledge, but equally to historical knowledge or any other kind I liked to name; and that it was foolish to think that one kind of knowledge could need a special epistemological study all to itself. I could see that they were mistaken; that in point of fact the thing they called theory of knowledge had been devised with special reference to the methodology of natural science; and that any one who attempted the 'application' of it to history found, if he knew what historical thinking was like, that no such application was possible. But perhaps I saw these things only because I knew where the shoe pinched. My head was already full of problems in historical methodology; so that, reviewing these problems one by one, I could ask myself 'what light do the accepted theories of knowledge throw on this? or on this? or on this?' and answer with certainty, every time, 'none'. It would have been unreasonable to expect a like certainty on the part of any one who had not already thought a great deal about historical method.

Even on the very modest ground that history was a form of intellectual activity on which, however inferior it might be in certainty, dignity, and utility to natural science, philosophy might do well to cast an eye, and that out of the thirty or forty professional philosophers in Oxford there would be no harm if one relegated himself to so obscure a province, it would have seemed worth my while to specialize, as I was perhaps unusually qualified for doing, in the study of historical method. Obscure provinces, like Roman Britain, always rather appeal to me. Their obscurity is a challenge; you have to invent new methods for studying them, and then you will probably find that the cause of their obscurity is some defect in the methods hitherto used. When these defects have been removed, it will be possible to revise the generally accepted opinions about other, more familiar, subjects, and to correct the errors with which those opinions are perhaps infected.

In this sense, knowledge advances by proceeding not 'from the known to the unknown', but from the 'unknown' to the 'known'. Obscure subjects, by forcing us to think harder and more systematically, sharpen our wits and thus enable us to dispel the fog of prejudice and superstition in which our minds are often wrapped when we think about what is familiar to us. The mere fact that historical methodology had been so completely neglected, at any rate in England, encouraged me to hope that by concentrating my attention upon it I might hit upon truths in the theory of knowledge which were concealed from the 'realists' by their obviously conventional and second-hand ideas about the methods of natural science.

For example, the current theories of 'scientific method' all agreed in making 'scientific' knowledge dependent on historical knowledge; though they were stated in such a way as to suggest that the writer hoped the reader would not notice it. No one, when he said that scientific knowledge depended on experiment, meant that a given scientific theory arose in a scientist's mind contemporaneously with the experiment (or rather, experiments) upon which it was based. He meant that a scientist, in framing a theory, made use of certain historical knowledge in his possession as to what experiments had been tried and what their results had been. It was a commonplace, though a concealed one, that all 'scientific' knowledge in this way involves an historical element; and it was clear to me that any philosopher who offered a theory of 'scientific method', without being in a position to offer a theory of historical method, was defrauding his public by supporting his world on an elephant and hoping that nobody would ask what kept the elephant up. It was no mere question of adding a theory of historical method to the already existing theory of 'scientific' method. It was a question of making good a defect in current theories of 'scientific' method by attending to an element in 'scientific' knowledge about which there seemed to be a conspiracy of silence, namely the historical element.

But there was more in my decision than that. In the last thirty or forty years historical thought had been achieving an acceleration in the velocity of its progress and an enlargement in its outlook comparable to those which natural science had achieved about the beginning of the seventeenth century. It seemed to me as nearly certain as anything in the future could be, that historical thought, whose constantly

increasing importance had been one of the most strik-
ing features of the nineteenth century, would increase
in importance far more rapidly during the twentieth;
and that we might very well be standing on the
threshold of an age in which history would be as
important for the world as natural science had been
between 1600 and 1900. If that was the case (and the
more I thought about it the likelier it seemed) the
wise philosopher would concentrate with all his might
on the problems of history, at whatever cost, and so
do his share in laying the foundations of the future.

IX

THE FOUNDATIONS OF THE FUTURE

I DID not exactly choose to spend the rest of my life on this task. By about 1919 I found that I had no choice but to do so. There was at that time a special reason, not so purely temporary as one might have hoped it to prove, why a man who felt himself able to do work of this kind should have wished to do it; and I will not deny that this reason weighed with me.

A war had just ended in which the destruction of life, the annihilation of property, and the disappointment of hopes for a peaceable and well-ordered international society, had surpassed all previous standards. What was worse, the intensity of the struggle seemed to have undermined, as if by the sheer force of the explosives it consumed, the moral energies of all the combatants; so that (I write as one who during the latter part of the war was employed in preparations for the peace conference) a war of unprecedented ferocity closed in a peace-settlement of unprecedented folly, in which statesmanship, even purely selfish statesmanship, was overwhelmed by the meanest and most idiotic passions. We had been warned some time ago, by Norman Angell, that in modern war there would be no victors in the sense that no party could be enriched by it; but we now learned that in another sense too there were no victors: no party whose morale rose superior to it; no group of statesmen who, by the end of it, had not become a mob of imbeciles, capable only of throwing away all the opportunities their soldiers had won them.

The War was an unprecedented triumph for natural science. Bacon had promised that knowledge would be power, and power it was: power to destroy the bodies and souls of men more rapidly than had ever been done by human agency before. This triumph paved the way to other triumphs: improvements in transport, in sanitation, in surgery, medicine, and psychiatry, in commerce and industry, and, above all, in preparations for the next war.

But in one way the War was an unprecedented disgrace to the human intellect. Whether it was deliberately plotted by a ring of German war-lords, as some believed, or by a ring of English trade-lords, as others believed, nobody has ever supposed that any except at most the tiniest fraction of the combatants wanted it. It happened because a situation got out of hand. As it went on, the situation got more and more out of hand. When the peace treaty was signed, it was more out of hand than ever. Fighting ended because one side was fought to a standstill, not because the situation was under control again.

The contrast between the success of modern European minds in controlling almost any situation in which the elements are physical bodies and the forces physical forces, and their inability to control situations in which the elements are human beings and the forces mental forces, left an indelible mark on the memory of every one who was concerned in it. I knew enough history to understand the force of the contrast. I knew that for sheer ineptitude the Versailles treaty surpassed previous treaties as much as for sheer technical excellence the equipment of twentieth-century armies surpassed those of previous armies. It seemed almost as if man's power to control 'Nature' had been increasing *pari passu* with a decrease in his power to control human affairs. That, I dare say, was an exaggeration. But it was a plain fact that the gigantic increase since about 1600 in his power to control Nature had not been accompanied by a corresponding increase, or anything like it, in his power to control human situations. And it was also a plain fact that the ill effects of any failure to control a human situation were more serious now than they had ever been before, in direct proportion to the magnitude of the new powers put by natural science, with divine indifference, into the hands of the evil and the good, the fool and the wise man. Not only would any failure to control human affairs result in more and more widespread destruction as natural science added triumph to triumph, but the consequences would tend more and more to the destruction of whatever was good and reasonable in the civilized world; for the evil would always begin using the engines of destruction before the good, the fool always before the wise man. I seemed to see the reign of natural science, within no very long time, converting Europe into a wilderness of Yahoos.

There was only one way in which this calamity could be averted; and only one in which, if it should occur, its effects could be repaired. European man's ability to control the forces of Nature was the fruit of three hundred years' investigation along the lines laid down early in the seventeenth century. It was the widening of the scientific outlook and the acceleration of scientific progress in the days of Galileo that had led in the fullness of time from the water-wheels and windmills of the Middle Ages to the almost incredible power and delicacy of the modern machine. In dealing with their fellow men, I could see, men were still what they were in dealing with machines in the Middle Ages. Well-meaning babblers talked about the necessity for a change of heart. But the trouble was obviously in the head. What was needed was not more goodwill and human affection, but more understanding of human affairs and more knowledge of how to handle them.

At this point in my thoughts the natural scientist would make a bid to restore his falling prestige. 'Why, yes,' said he; 'everything you have said is true; what we must have, if civilization is to be saved, is a thorough knowledge of human affairs. And that means a thorough knowledge of the human mind and its various processes, and of the different forms which these processes take in the various types of human beings. Like all genuine knowledge, this must be scientific knowledge; in a word, it must be psychology. Psychology, the science which, young though it is, has already exploded the pretensions and inherited the possessions of the old pseudo-sciences of logic, ethics, political theory, and so forth, is the saviour that the world is seeking.'

If this claim never for a moment deceived me, that is a benefit I owed to my early studies in theology. Like every one else who studied that subject in those days, I read William James's *Varieties of Religious Experience* and a lot of other books in which religion was treated from a psychological point of view. If I was profoundly shocked by the *Varieties*, that was not because some of the facts described in it were such as I would rather not hear about. They were, on the whole, amusing. Nor was it because I thought James was doing his work clumsily. I thought he did it very well. It was because the whole thing was a fraud. The book professed to throw light on a certain subject, and threw on it no light whatever. And that because of the method used. It was not because the book was a bad example of psychology, but because it was a good example of psychology, that it left its subject completely unilluminated. And in *Religion and Philosophy* I attacked, not William James, but any and every psychological treatment of religion, in a passage of which the crucial words are 'the mind, regarded in this way, ceases to be a mind at all'.

This piece of work now stood me in good stead. It was easy to see that any attempt to bring ethics within the field of psychology (and attempts of that kind had been made often enough), or to do the same with politics, would necessarily and always result in failure. As I knew very well, the plea 'do not criticize this science; it is in its infancy', rested on a falsehood. Psychology was very far from being a young science; both word and thing had been in existence ever since

the sixteenth century. It was not only an old-estab-
lished science, it had for centuries been a respectable
and even a neighbourly one. It had been deliberately
created, as any one might guess who knew enough
Greek to understand its name, in order to study that
which is neither mind in the proper traditional sense
(consciousness, reason, will) nor yet body, but ψυχή, or
such functions as sensation and appetite. It marched
on the one hand with physiology, and on the other with
the sciences of mind proper, logic and ethics, the
sciences of reason and will. And it showed no desire
to encroach on its neighbours' territories until, early
in the nineteenth century, the dogma got about that
reason and will were only concretions of sense and
appetite. If that was so, it followed that logic and
ethics could disappear, and that their functions could
be taken over by psychology. For there was no such
thing as 'mind'; what had been so called was only
'psyche'.

That is what underlies the modern pretence that
psychology can deal with what once were called the
problems of logic and ethics, and the modern claim
of psychology to be a science of mind. People who
make or admit that claim ought to know what it implies. It implies the systematic abolition of all those
distinctions which, being valid for reason and will but
not for sensation and appetite, constitute the special
subject-matter of logic and ethics: distinctions like
that between truth and error, knowledge and ignorance, science and sophistry, right and wrong, good
and bad, expedient and inexpedient. Distinctions of

this kind form the armature of every science; no one can abolish them and remain a scientist; psychology, therefore, regarded as the science of mind, is not a science. It is what 'phrenology' was in the early nineteenth century, and astrology and alchemy in the Middle Ages and the sixteenth century: the fashionable scientific fraud of the age.

These observations implied no hostility towards psychology proper, the science of sensation, appetite, and the emotions connected with them, or towards the Freudian and other forms of treatment for certain ailments, of which we were beginning to hear a good deal, and to which later I devoted a good deal of attention. At the time of which I am speaking Freud was only a name to me. But when I came to study his works I was not unprepared for the discovery that they reached a very high scientific level when dealing with problems in psychotherapy, but sank beneath contempt when they treated of ethics, politics, religion, or social structure. Nor was it strange that Freud's imitators and rivals, less intelligent and less conscientious writers whom I will not name, reached on these subjects an even lower level.

Was it possible that men should come to a better understanding of human affairs by studying history? Was history the thing which in future might play a part in civilized life analogous to that of natural science in the past? Obviously not, if history was only a scissors-and-paste affair. If historians could only repeat, with different arrangements and different styles of decoration, what others had said before them, the age-old hope of using it as a school of political wisdom was as vain as Hegel knew it to be when he made his famous remark that the only thing to be learnt from history is that nobody ever learns anything from history.

But what if history is not a scissors-and-paste affair? What if the historian resembles the natural scientist in asking his own questions, and insisting on an answer? Clearly, that altered the situation. But might he not ask questions whose answers, however interesting, were of no practical use?

The historian is a person whose questions are about the past. He is generally supposed to be a person whose questions are exclusively about the past; about a past, namely, that is dead and gone, and in no sense at all living on into the present. I had not gone very far in my study of historical thought before I realized that this was a delusion. The historian cannot answer questions about the past unless he has evidence about it. His evidence, if he 'has' it, must be something existing here and now in his present world. If there were a past event which had left no trace of any kind in the present world, it would be a past event for which now there was no evidence, and nobody—no historian; I say nothing of other, perhaps more highly gifted, persons—could know anything about it.

In order that a past event should have left in the present world a 'trace' of itself which to the historian is evidence for it, this trace must be something more than any material body, or any state of a material body. Suppose a medieval king granted certain land to a certain monastery, and suppose the charter recording the grant is preserved to this day, a brown piece of parchment covered with certain black marks. The only reason why this parchment can serve to a modern historian as evidence of the grant is because other things, besides the parchment, survive from the medieval world into the world of to-day. To take only one of these things, the knowledge of Latin survives. Other indispensable survivals, of the same general type, will occur to every reader. I will confine myself to the one I have mentioned. If the habit of reading and understanding Latin had not survived among 'clerkly' persons from the Middle Ages to the present day, the parchment could never have told the historian what in fact it does tell him. In general terms, the modern historian can study the Middle Ages, in the way in which he actually does study them, only because they are not dead. By that I mean not that their writings and so forth are still in existence as material objects, but that their ways of thinking are still in existence as ways in which people still think. The survival need not be continuous. Such things may have died and been raised from the dead, like the ancient languages of Mesopotamia and Egypt.

By about 1920 this was my first principle of a philosophy of history: that the past which an historian studies is not a dead past, but a past which in some sense is still living in the present. At the time, I expressed this by saying that history is concerned not with 'events' but with 'processes'; that 'processes' are things which do not begin and end but turn into one another; and that if a process P_1 turns into a process P_2, there is no dividing line at which P_1 stops and P_2 begins; P_1 never stops, it goes on in the changed form P_2, and P_2 never begins, it has previously been going on in the earlier form P_1. There are in history no beginnings and no endings. History books begin and end, but the events they describe do not.

If P_1 has left traces of itself in P_2 so that an historian living in P_2 can discover by the interpretation of evidence that what is now P_2 was once P_1, it follows that the 'traces' of P_1 in the present are not, so to speak, the corpse of a dead P_1 but rather the real P_1 itself, living and active though incapsulated within the other form of itself P_2. And P_2 is not opaque, it is transparent, so that P_1 shines through it and their colours combine into one. Therefore, if the symbol P_1 stands for a characteristic of a certain historical period and the symbol P_2 for the corresponding but different (and therefore contradictory or incompatible) characteristic of its successor, that successor is never characterized by P_2 pure and simple, but always by a P_2 tinged with a survival of P_1. This is why people who try to depict the characteristic features of this or that historical period go wrong if they do their work too thoroughly, forgetting that the silk of their period is in reality always a shot silk, combining in itself contradictory colours.

The idea of a living past, together with a good many others connected with it, I had completely worked out by 1920; and in that year I wrote them down in an essay of short book-length, very sparing of words and making point after point without any attempt at elaboration or explanation. It was primarily a study of the nature and implications of process or becoming. Secondarily, it was an attack on 'realism', showing how the *non possumus* of 'realists' towards a theory of history arose from their refusal to admit the reality of becoming, and from their analysis of the true proposition 'P_1 becomes P_2' into the complex of propositions 'P_1 is P_1', 'P_1 is not P_2', 'P_1 ends where P_2 begins', 'P_2 is P_2', and 'P_2 is not P_1', all of them either tautologous or false. This book, written in three days, was intended only to help the process of crystallization in my own thoughts; it would have been quite unintelligible to the general public, and I never contemplated printing it. Nobody has seen it except my friend Guido de Ruggiero, for whom I typed a copy, thinking that it might amuse him as an historian of philosophy.[1] By way of a private joke, I called it *Libellus de Generatione*, and prefixed to it a motto: 'For as the old hermit of Prague, that never saw pen and ink, very wittily said to a niece of king Gorboduc, That, that is, is: for what is that, but that? and is, but is?'

How, I asked, did these conceptions affect the question whether history could be a school of moral and political wisdom? The old pragmatic idea of history was futile because its idea of history was the scissors-and-paste idea in which the past is a dead past, and knowing about it means only knowing what the authorities say about it. And that knowledge is useless as a

---

[1] The original manuscript, like the only manuscript of *Truth and Contradiction*, was destroyed after I wrote this book.

guide to action; because, since history never exactly repeats itself, the problem before me now is never sufficiently like the problem described by my authorities to justify me in repeating the solution which then succeeded, or avoiding that which then failed. So long as the past and present are outside one another, knowledge of the past is not of much use in the problems of the present. But suppose the past lives on in the present; suppose, though incapsulated in it, and at first sight hidden beneath the present's contradictory and more prominent features, it is still alive and active; then the historian may very well be related to the non-historian as the trained woodsman is to the ignorant traveller. 'Nothing here but trees and grass', thinks the traveller, and marches on. 'Look,' says the woodsman, 'there is a tiger in that grass.' The historian's business is to reveal the less obvious features hidden from a careless eye in the present situation. What history can bring to moral and political life is a trained eye for the situation in which one has to act.

This may seem a small gift. Surely, some one will say, we are entitled to ask for more than that. There is not much use in showing us the tiger unless you also give us a rifle with which to shoot him. The historian will not do very much to help us in our moral and political difficulties if he only makes us see the features of the situation and does not also provide us with rules for acting in situations of that kind.

There were two things, it seemed to me, which needed to be said in answer to that. The first can be said quite shortly, but I thought it did not wholly cover the ground; for a complete answer, the second had to be said as well, and that could only be said at greater length. I will say them both.

The first is this. You want a rifle? Then go where rifles are to be had. Go to the gunsmith's. But do not expect the gunsmith to sell you a rifle which can see tigers as well as shoot them. For that, you must learn woodcraft.

In other words: if ready-made rules for dealing with situations of specific types are what you want, natural science is the kind of thing which can provide them. The reason why the civilization of 1600–1900, based upon natural science, found bankruptcy staring it in the face was because, in its passion for ready-made rules, it had neglected to develop that kind of insight which alone could tell it what rules to apply, not in a situation of a specific type, but in the situation in which it actually found itself. It was precisely because history offered us something altogether different from rules, namely insight, that it could afford us the help we needed in diagnosing our moral and political problems.

The second is this. If you are sure that the thing you are going to see in the grass is going to be a tiger, and if your only idea about tigers is that they are things to shoot, take a rifle with you. But are you sure? What if it turns out to be your own child playing Indians?

In other words: there are situations which, for one reason or another, can be handled without appeal to any ready-made rules at all, so long as you have insight into them. All you need in such cases is to see what the situation is, and you can then extemporize a way of dealing with it which will prove satisfactory. This second type of case, I thought, was of great importance in moral and political life, and I will explain as best I can, though I cannot do so very briefly, what I was thinking about it.

When I speak of action, I shall be referring to that kind of action in which the agent does what he does not because he is in a certain situation, but because he knows or believes himself to be in a certain situation. I shall not be referring to any kind of action which arises as a mere response to stimuli which the situation may contain, or as the mere effect of the agent's nature or disposition or temporary state. And when I speak of action according to rule, I shall be referring to that kind of action in which the agent, knowing or believing that there is a certain rule, applicable to the situation in which he knows or believes himself to be, decides to act in accordance with it. I shall not be referring to any kind of action in which the agent, though actually obeying a rule, is unaware that he is doing so.

In a great part of our actions we act according to rules, and that is what makes our action successful. This is because we are moving among situations of certain standard types, and trying to manipulate them so as to obtain certain standard results. Action according to rule is a very important kind of action, and the first question which any intelligent man asks, when he finds himself in a situation of any kind, is 'What are the rules for acting in this kind of situation?'

But although action according to rules is a very important kind of action, it is not the only kind. There are two kinds of occasions on which another kind is necessary. Before describing them, I will try to show that it exists.

Suppose you find yourself in a situation of a given type S; and suppose you want to obtain a result of a given type R, and there is a rule that in a situation of type S the way to get a result of a type R is to do an action of type A. You may know this rule, but how do you know it? Either because of your own experience or because of some one else's. In either case a certain body of experience has been accumulated before the rule could be known to any one. This experience must have been experience of acting in situations of the type S by persons who wanted to obtain results of the type R but did not know the rule. And their endeavours to obtain results of type R must often have been successful; otherwise the experience which led to the formulation of the rule could never have accumulated. There must, therefore, be a kind of action which is not determined according to rule, and where the process is directly from knowledge of the situation to an action appropriate to that situation, without passing through the stage of formulating a rule appropriate to the situation. And it must be very common, for a vast deal of it must go to the formulation of even the most trivial rule of conduct.

(1) The first kind of occasion on which it is necessary to act without rules is when you find yourself in a situation that you do not recognize as belonging to

any of your known types. No rule can tell you how to act. But you cannot refrain from acting. No one is ever free to act or not to act, at his own discretion. *Il faut parier*, as Pascal said. You must do something. Here are you, up against this situation: you must improvise as best you can a method of handling it.

(2) The second kind of occasion on which you must act without rules is when you can refer the situation to a known type, but are not content to do so. You know a rule for dealing with situations of this kind, but you are not content with applying it, because you know that action according to rules always involves a certain misfit between yourself and your situation. If you act according to rules, you are not dealing with the situation in which you stand, you are only dealing with a certain type of situation under which you class it. The type is, admittedly, a useful handle with which to grasp the situation; but all the same, it comes between you and the situation it enables you to grasp. Often enough, that does not matter; but sometimes it matters very much.

Thus everybody has certain rules according to which he acts in dealing with his tailor. These rules are, we will grant, soundly based on genuine experience; and by acting on them a man will deal fairly with his tailor and helps his tailor to deal fairly by him. But so far as he acts according to these rules, he is dealing with his tailor only in his capacity as a tailor, not as John Robinson, aged sixty, with a weak heart and a consumptive daughter, a passion for gardening and an overdraft at the bank. The rules for dealing with tailors no doubt enable you to cope with the tailor in John Robinson, but they prevent you from getting to grips with whatever else there may be in him. Of course, if you know that he has a weak heart, you will manage your dealings with him by modifying the rules for tailor-situations in the light of the rules for situations involving people with weak hearts. But at this rate the modifications soon become so complicated that the rules are no longer of any practical use to you. You have got beyond the stage at which rules can guide action, and you go back to improvising, as best you can, a method of handling the situation in which you find yourself.

Of these two cases in which it is necessary to act otherwise than according to rule, the first arises out of the agent's inexperience and ignorance of life. It is commonest, therefore, in the young, and in all of us when, owing to travel or some other disturbance of our regular routine, we find ourselves in unfamiliar surroundings. The second arises only for people of experience and intelligence, and even then occurs only when they take a situation very seriously; so seriously as to reject not only the claims of that almost undisguised tempter Desire, and that thinly disguised one Self-Interest, but (a tempter whose disguise is so good that most people hardly ever penetrate it at all and, if they do, suffer the sincerest remorse afterwards) Right Conduct, or action according to the recognized rules.

From this point of view I could see that any one who asked for rules, in order to obtain from them instruction how to act, was clinging to the low-grade morality of custom and precept. He was trying to see only those elements in the situation which he already knew how to deal with, and was shutting his eyes to anything which might convince him that his ready-made rules were not an adequate guide to the conduct of life.

Rules of conduct kept action at a low potential, because they involved a certain blindness to the realities of the situation. If action was to be raised to a higher potential, the agent must open his eyes wider and see more clearly the situation in which he was acting. If the function of history was to inform people about the past, where the past was understood as a dead past, it could do very little towards helping them to act; but if its function was to inform them about the present, in so far as the past, its ostensible subject-matter, was incapsulated in the present and constituted a part of it not at once obvious to the untrained eye, then history stood in the closest possible relation to practical life. Scissors-and-paste history, with its ideal of obtaining from authorities ready-made information about a dead past, obviously could not teach man to control human situations as natural science had taught him to control the forces of Nature; nor could any such distilled essence of scissors-and-paste history as had been proposed by Auguste Comte under the name of sociology; but there seemed to be some chance that the new kind of history might prove able to do so.

X

HISTORY AS THE SELF-KNOWLEDGE OF MIND

THIS chance became a probability as soon as my conception of history had advanced another step forward. This step was taken, or rather registered, in 1928, when I spent a vacation at Le Martouret, that pleasant country-house near Die, sitting under the plane-trees on the terrace and writing down as shortly as I could the lessons of my last nine years' work in historical research and reflection upon it. It is difficult to believe that so obvious a point was reached so slowly; but the evidence of my manuscripts is clear; and I know that I have always been a slow and painful thinker, in whom thought in its formative stages will not be hurried by effort, nor clarified by argument, that most dangerous enemy to immature thoughts, but grows obscurely through a long and oppressive period of gestation, and only after birth can be licked by its parent into presentable shape.

It was in my Die manuscript that I first drew the distinction between history proper and what I called pseudo-history. By that name I referred to such things as the narratives of geology, palaeontology, astronomy, and other natural sciences which in the late eighteenth and the nineteenth centuries had assumed a semblance at least of historicity. Reflection on my experience as an archaeologist enabled me to see that this was no more than a semblance. Archaeologists had often called attention to the likeness between their own stratigraphical methods and those of geology, and a likeness there certainly was; but there was a difference as well.

If an archaeologist finds a stratum of earth and stones and mortar, mixed with potsherds and coins, on the top of which is a layer of level flags, supporting more earth with potsherds and coins of a rather different type, it is easy to say that he uses these two sets of potsherds and coins exactly as a geologist uses fossils, to show that the strata belong to different periods and to date them by correlating them with strata found elsewhere and containing relics of the same type.

Easy, but untrue. For the archaeologist, these things are not stone and clay and metal, they are building-stone and potsherds and coins; debris of a building, fragments of domestic utensils, and means of exchange, all belonging to a bygone age whose purposes they reveal to him. He can use them as historical evidence only so far as he understands what each one of them was for. If in the case of one object he does not understand that, he has, as an archaeologist, no use for the object; he would throw it away, but that he hopes some one more learned or more resourceful than himself may solve the riddle. It is not only the minutiae, like pins and buttons, that he regards as expressions of purpose; he thinks of the whole building, the whole settlement, in the same way.

Before the nineteenth century, a natural scientist might have replied that the same was true of his own studies: was not every task in natural science a contribution to the decipherment of the purposes of that mighty being whom some called Nature and others God? The nineteenth-century scientist would answer quite firmly that it was not. And the nineteenth-century scientist is right as to the facts. Natural science as it exists to-day, and has existed for the best part of a century, does not include the idea of purpose among its working categories. Perhaps he is right in his theology too. I cannot think it pious to make our study of Nature depend on the assumption that the purposes of God are within our grasp; and if a palaeontologist told me that he never bothered to ask what trilobites were for, I should be glad, for the sake of his immortal soul as well as the progress of his science. If archaeology and palaeontology worked according to the same principles, trilobites would be as valueless to that palaeontologist as are to the archaeologist those 'iron implements of uncertain use' which cause him so much embarrassment.

History and pseudo-history alike consisted of narratives: but in history these were narratives of pur-posive activity, and the evidence for them consisted of relics they had left behind (books or potsherds, the principle was the same) which became evidence precisely to the extent to which the historian con-ceived them in terms of purpose, that is, understood what they were for; in pseudo-history there is no con-ception of purpose, there are only relics of various kinds, differing among themselves in such ways that they have to be interpreted as relics of different pasts which can be arranged on a time-scale.

I expressed this new conception of history in the phrase: 'all history is the history of thought.' You are thinking historically, I meant, when you say about anything, 'I see what the person who made this (wrote this, used this, designed this, &c.) was thinking.' Until you can say that, you may be trying to think historically but you are not succeeding. And there is nothing else except thought that can be the object of historical knowledge. Political history is the history of political thought: not 'political theory', but the thought which occupies the mind of a man engaged in political work: the formation of a policy, the planning of means to execute it, the attempt to carry it into effect, the discovery that others are hostile to it, the devising of ways to overcome their hostility, and so forth. Consider how the historian describes a famous speech. He does not concern himself with any sensuous elements in it such as the pitch of the statesman's voice, the hardness of the benches, the deafness of the old gentleman in the third row: he concentrates his attention on what the man was trying to say (the thought, that is, expressed in his words) and how his audience received it (the thoughts in their minds, and how these conditioned the impact upon them of the statesman's thought). Military history, again, is not a description of weary marches in heat or cold, or the thrills and chills of battle or the long agony of wounded men. It is a description of plans and counter-plans: of thinking about strategy and thinking about tactics, and in the last resort of what the men in the ranks thought about the battle.

On what conditions was it possible to know the history of a thought? First, the thought must be expressed: either in what we call language, or in one of the many other forms of expressive activity. Historical painters seem to regard an outstretched arm and a pointing hand as the characteristic gesture expressing the thought of a commanding officer. Running away expresses the thought that all hope of victory is gone. Secondly, the historian must be able to think over again for himself the thought whose expression he is trying to interpret. If for any reason he is such a kind of man that he cannot do this, he had better leave that problem alone. The important point here is that the historian of a certain thought must think for himself that very same thought, not another like it. If some one, hereinafter called the mathematician, has written that twice two is four, and if some one else, hereinafter called the historian, wants to know what he was thinking when he made those marks on paper, the historian will never be able to answer this question unless he is mathematician enough to think exactly what the mathematician thought, and expressed by writing that twice two are four. When he interprets the marks on paper, and says, 'by these marks the mathematician meant that twice two are four', he is thinking simultaneously: (a) that twice two are four, (b) that the mathematician thought this, too; and (c) that he expressed this thought by making these marks on paper. I will not offer to help a reader who replies, 'ah, you are making it easy for yourself by taking an example where history really is the history of thought; you couldn't explain the history of a battle or a political campaign in that way.' I could, and so could you, Reader, if you tried.

This gave me a second proposition: 'historical knowledge is the re-enactment in the historian's mind of the thought whose history he is studying.'

When I understand what Nelson meant by saying, 'in honour I won them, in honour I will die with them', what I am doing is to think myself into the position of being all covered with decorations and exposed at short range to the musketeers in the enemy's tops, and being advised to make myself a less conspicuous target. I ask myself the question, shall I change my coat? and reply in those words. Understanding the words means thinking for myself what Nelson thought when he spoke them: that this is not a time to take off my ornaments of honour for the sake of saving my life. Unless I were capable—perhaps only transiently—of thinking that for myself, Nelson's words would remain meaningless to me; I could only weave a net of verbiage round them like a psychologist, and talk about masochism and guilt-sense, or introversion and extraversion, or some such foolery.

But this re-enactment of Nelson's thought is a re-enactment with a difference. Nelson's thought, as Nelson thought it and as I re-think it, is certainly one and the same thought; and yet in some way there is not one thought, there are two different thoughts. What was the difference? No question in my study of historical method ever gave me so much trouble; and the answer was not complete until some years later.

The difference is one of context. To Nelson, that thought was a present thought; to me, it is a past thought living in the present but (as I have elsewhere put it) incapsulated, not free. What is an incapsulated thought? It is a thought which, though perfectly alive, forms no part of the question–answer complex which constitutes what people call the 'real' life, the superficial or obvious present, of the mind in question. For myself, or for that which at first sight I regard as myself, the question 'shall I take off my decorations?' does not arise. The questions that arise are, for example, 'shall I go on reading this book?' and later, 'what did the *Victory*'s deck look like to a person thinking about his chances of surviving the battle?' and later again, 'what should I have done if I had been in Nelson's place?' No question that arises in this primary series, the series constituting my 'real' life, ever requires the answer 'in honour I won them, in honour I will die with them'. But a question arising in that primary series may act as a switch into another dimension. I plunge beneath the surface of my mind, and there live a life in which I not merely think about Nelson but am Nelson, and thus in thinking about Nelson think about myself. But this secondary life is prevented from overflowing into my primary life by being what I call incapsulated, that is, existing in a context of primary or surface knowledge which keeps it in its place and prevents it from thus overflowing. Such knowledge, I mean, as that Trafalgar happened ninety years ago: I am a little boy in a jersey: this is my father's study carpet, not the

Atlantic, and that the study fender, not the coast of Spain.

So I reached my third proposition: 'Historical knowledge is the re-enactment of a past thought in-capsulated in a context of present thoughts which, by contradicting it, confine it to a plane different from theirs.'

How is one to know which of these planes is 'real' life, and which mere 'history'? By watching the way in which historical problems arise. Every historical problem ultimately arises out of 'real' life. The scis-sors-and-paste men think differently: they think that first of all people get into the habit of reading books, and then the books put questions into their heads. But I am not talking about scissors-and-paste history. In the kind of history that I am thinking of, the kind I have been practising all my life, historical problems arise out of practical problems. We study history in order to see more clearly into the situation in which we are called upon to act. Hence the plane on which, ultimately, all problems arise is the plane of 'real' life: that to which they are referred for their solution is history.

If what the historian knows is past thoughts, and if he knows them by re-thinking them himself, it follows that the knowledge he achieves by historical inquiry is not knowledge of his situation as opposed to know-ledge of himself, it is a knowledge of his situation which is at the same time knowledge of himself. In re-thinking what somebody else thought, he thinks it himself. In knowing that somebody else thought it,

he knows that he himself is able to think it. And finding out what he is able to do is finding out what kind
of a man he is. If he is able to understand, by re-
thinking them, the thoughts of a great many different
kinds of people, it follows that he must be a great
many kinds of man. He must be, in fact, a microcosm
of all the history he can know. Thus his own self-
knowledge is at the same time his knowledge of the
world of human affairs.

This train of thought was not complete until about
1930. By completing it, I completed my answer to the
question that had haunted me ever since the War. How
could we construct a science of human affairs, so to
call it, from which men could learn to deal with human
situations as skilfully as natural science had taught
them to deal with situations in the world of Nature?
The answer was now clear and certain. The science
of human affairs was history. This was a discovery
which could not have been made before the late nineteenth century, for it was not until then that history
began to undergo a Baconian revolution, to emerge
from the chrysalis of its scissors-and-paste stage, and
thus to become, in the proper sense of that word, a
science. It was because history was still in the chrysalis stage in the eighteenth century, that eighteenth-
century thinkers, when they saw the need for a science
of human affairs, could not identify it with history but
tried to realize it in the shape of a 'science of human
nature'; which, as men like Hume conceived it, with
its strictly empirical methods, was in effect an historical study of the contemporary European mind,

falsified by the assumption that human minds had everywhere and at all times worked like those of eighteenth-century Europeans. The nineteenth century, likewise in search of a science of human affairs, tried to realize it in the shape of a 'psychology' in which the mental was reduced to the psychical, the distinction between truth and falsehood thrown overboard, and the very idea of a science negated, psychology itself being involved in the resulting bankruptcy. But the revolution in historical method which had superseded scissors-and-paste history by what I called history proper had swept away these sham sciences and had brought into existence a genuine, actual, visibly and rapidly progressing form of knowledge which now for the first time was putting man in a position to obey the oracular precept 'know thyself', and to reap the benefits that only such obedience could confer.

The ideas very briefly summarized in this chapter and the two preceding it were being worked out for nearly twenty years after I became a teacher of philosophy. They were repeatedly written down, corrected, and rewritten; for whenever I have had a cub to lick into shape, my pen is the only tongue I have found useful. None of these writings has ever been intended for publication,[1] although much of their

[1] Points out of them might have been published piecemeal in short articles, and now and then I did print such articles; but the only place for them was in philosophical periodicals, where they were rendered useless by the fixed determination of the persons who read such periodicals not to think about history. When I was elected to the British Academy in 1934, and was invited to contribute to their *Proceedings*, I found a more open-minded audience,

substance has been repeatedly given in lecture form; but I am publishing this short summary because the main problems are now solved, and publishing them in full is only a question of time and health.

Thinking them out was laborious, because of the method used. Every detail arose out of reflection on actual historical research, in which I had therefore to be incessantly engaged, and was tested over and over again by fresh pieces of research devised to that end. By about 1930 my health was beginning to suffer from long-continued overwork. Whether luckily or unluckily, I have never known any illness interfere with my power of thinking and writing, or with the quality of what I think and write. When I am unwell, I have only to begin work on some piece of philosophical writing, and all my ailments are forgotten until I leave off. But this does not cure them. If they are due to overwork, it may aggravate them.

They were further aggravated by my growing inability to resist involvement in various departments of University business. In this way I slaked my passion for administrative work, until I discovered that this, too, was only another arc of the vicious circle.

By this time I had in my head a great deal which I believed the public would value; and the only way of giving it to the public was by writing books. On this, therefore, I decided to spend my leisure; and planned a series, to begin with an *Essay on Philosophical Method*.

and wrote them a paper on 'Human Nature and Human History' (*Proc. Brit. Acad.*, xxii) in which some of the ideas referred to in this chapter are discussed.

This I wrote during a long illness in 1932. It is my best book in matter; in style, I may call it my only book, for it is the only one I ever had the time to finish as well as I knew how, instead of leaving it in a more or less rough state. After settling accounts with my archaeological studies in a way to be described in the next chapter, I wrote in 1937 the second book of my series, *The Principles of Art*.[1] Before it had gone through the press I was overtaken by the more serious illness which gave me both the leisure and the motive to write this autobiography; whose purpose is to put on record some brief account of the work I have not yet been able to publish, in case I am not able to publish it in full.

Henceforth I shall spend all my available time in going on with the series. I am nearly fifty, and cannot in any case hope for more than a few years in which I can do my best work. I take this opportunity, therefore, of saying that I will not be drawn into discussion of what I write. Some readers may wish to convince me that it is all nonsense. I know how they would do it; I could invent their criticisms for myself. Some may wish to show me that on this or that detail I am wrong. Perhaps I am; if they are in a position to prove it, let them write not about me but about the subject, showing that they can write about it better than I can; and I will read them gladly. And if there are any who

[1] I say nothing about the motives which led me to work at the philosophy of art, the process of training by which I qualified myself for that work, or the way in which my thoughts about it progressed during long years. A reader can find out all he needs to know on these subjects from *The Principles of Art* itself.

think my work good, let them show their approval of it by attention to their own. So, perhaps, I may escape otherwise than by death the last humiliation of an aged scholar, when his juniors conspire to print a volume of essays and offer it to him as a sign that they now consider him senile.

XI

ROMAN BRITAIN

IT was necessary for the advancement of my philosophical work that I should be constantly engaged not only in philosophical studies but in historical studies as well; and in a field where I could initiate lines of research in which I could hope for the co-operation of others; a field, therefore, in which I was an acknowledged master. The field had, accordingly, to be a small one, and ripe for intensive cultivation. For this purpose Roman Britain was very suitable. Moreover, I was already committed. Haverfield, the great master of the subject, died in 1919; most of his pupils had already fallen in the War; I was left the only man resident in Oxford whom he had trained as a Romano-British specialist; and even if my philosophy had not demanded it, I should have thought myself, in piety to him, under an obligation to keep alive the Oxford school of Romano-British studies that he had founded, to pass on the training he had given me, and to make use of the specialist library he had left to the University. It was this obligation that made me refuse all offers of professorships and other employments elsewhere which I received during the years that followed the War.

My first book dealing with the subject as a whole was written in 1921, at the invitation of the Delegates of the Clarendon Press. It was a short book; I wrote it in two days; it was designed to be elementary, and it was full of faults. However, it served to lay down once for all my general attitude towards the problems, and, even more important, my general conception (partly due to Haverfield, but partly different from his) of what the problems were; it gave me a first opportunity of finding out, more clearly than was possible within the limits of a short article, how my conception of historical research was developing; and by its sale it proved the liveliness of the welcome which the public was prepared to give to that idea. Ten years later I rewrote it in an enlarged edition, and had to revise that again in 1934. In the same year I wrote the British section in Professor Tenney Frank's *Economic Survey of Ancient Rome*, and in 1935 the sections of the *Oxford History of England* on prehistoric and Roman Britain, J. N. L. Myres writing a section on the English settlements, and these together making up the first volume.

The invitations to write these two large-scale works came at exactly the right moment. I had been long enough in my laboratory; I wanted to exchange it for my study. It was time to begin arranging and publishing the lessons which all this archaeological and historical work had taught me about the philosophy of history. But I could not desert Roman Britain without saying good-bye; and a full-length book about it would not only do that, it would serve to display in a concrete form the principles of historical thinking as I now understood them.

Most of these principles were, more or less unconsciously, common ground among historians; but not all of them were generally accepted; or perhaps it would be truer to say that comparatively few were consciously recognized, and of those by no means all were generally regarded as principles by which the historian ought to stand firm through thick and thin.

For example, long practice in excavation had taught me that one condition—indeed the most important condition—of success was that the person responsible for any piece of digging, however small and however large, should know exactly why he was doing it. He must first of all decide what he wants to find out, and then decide what kind of digging will show it to him. This was the central principle of my 'logic of question and answer' as applied to archaeology. In the beginnings of archaeology digging had been done blindly, that is, without any definite question to which an answer was being sought. A landowner with intellectual interests had dug an ancient site because it was on his land; and he dug it with no problem in his head, only the vague formula 'Let us see what objects of interest we can find here for my collection', or, when the curiosity-hunger of the eighteenth-century antiquary had given way to the knowledge-hunger of his nineteenth-century successor, 'Let us see what we can find out about this site'; which is no more a 'question', as I understand that term, than are such pseudo-questions as 'What is knowledge?' 'What is duty?' 'What is the *summum bonum*?' 'What is art?' Like them, it is only a vague portmanteau-phrase covering a multitude of possible questions but not precisely expressing any of them.

In our own days, when the enlightened landowner with money to spare is an almost extinct species, excavation is organized by local societies, directed by expert archaeologists, and paid for by public subscription. Although things have changed in all these respects, they have not changed in the one that is important. Most of our digging is still 'blind' digging. The public (including persons of all grades of wealth, from rich bankers and industrialists downward) cares little or nothing for historical knowledge. If you want a lever to extract money from the public for an excavation, you must not tell them that it will yield a solution for important historical problems. Natural scientists can say that kind of thing, because after three centuries of propaganda they have battered a way for it into the public's skull. But archaeologists have to use as their lever that nostalgic self-loathing which is so characteristic of our times. 'Here is a romantic ancient site', they must say, 'which is about to be covered with revolting bungalows, hideous by-pass roads, and so forth. Give us your guineas, so that we can find whatever is to be found there before our chance is gone for ever.' Thus, instead of being chosen for excavation because it contains the solution of a burning problem, a site is excavated for non-scientific reasons, exactly as in the old days.

Other sites are excavated because the local antiquaries have long wanted to dig them but have been prevented by refusal of leave on the part of their owners. Then arises an owner who gives his consent; and the local antiquaries snatch at their opportunity, and go to the public for subscriptions while the going is good. Others, again, because they lie not in a rich man's park but in a strong antiquarian society's district; while others, in the district of a society which is either weaker or less interested in things of that special kind, lie untouched.

If historical studies were to pass through a Baconian revolution—the revolution which converts a blind and random study into one where definite questions are asked and definite answers insisted upon—the first thing to be done was to preach that revolution among the historians themselves. When I began to study Roman Britain the revolution had made a little progress, but not much. Haverfield and his colleagues of the Cumberland Excavation Committee in the eighteen-nineties had been consciously and completely Baconian in their methods. They never dug a trench without knowing exactly what information they were looking for; they knew both that this information was the next thing they needed for the progress of their study, and also that this trench would give it them. That is why they could settle highly intricate and abstruse problems at a cost of never more, and often much less, than thirty or forty pounds a year. And their successors in the north adopted and continued to apply their principles.

But in the south, when I began to frequent the rooms of the Society of Antiquaries, I found a very different state of things. Excavation was still being done according to the principles laid down by General Pitt-Rivers in the last quarter of the nineteenth century. Pitt-Rivers was a very great archaeologist and a supreme master in the technique of excavation; but as regards the problems to be solved by excavation he was for the most part (not quite consistently) in the pre-Baconian stage. He dug in order to see what he could find out. He had not applied to archaeology the famous advice of Lord Acton, 'study problems, not periods'. Among his successors, as I found, archaeology meant studying not problems but sites. The idea of excavation was to choose a site: to uncover it systematically, one piece each year, pouring thousands of pounds into the work, until it was all dug; and then go on to another. The result was that, although museums were choked with the finds, amazingly little (as it now appears) was discovered about the history of the site. The Society of Antiquaries had excavated Silchester in this style for twenty years running; and although long before the end of that time the principles of stratigraphical digging were familiar even to the general public, and the dating of strata on Roman sites by coins and pottery was a well-established practice, the Silchester excavations fixed the date neither of the town's beginning nor of its end, nor of the walls nor of the street-plan, nor of a single house or public building, nor even of any alteration carried out to a house or public building. The analysis of the bath-building into work of several different periods remains a model of its kind, except for the fact that not one of these periods was dated; so that the whole analysis is historically useless. Phases in the occupation of this or that house which can now be dated, on the evidence of parallels elsewhere, to the fourth century or even the third, were ascribed by pure guess-work to 'wandering herdsmen' of the Dark Ages.

Things have changed since then, and I will not say that they have changed because of my efforts. But I will say that, for nearer twenty years than ten, I have been preaching to my archaeological friends the duty of never digging either a five-thousand-pound site or a five-shilling trench without being certain that you can satisfy an inquirer who asks you 'What are you doing this piece of work for?' And I will say that, at first, this idea was much ridiculed by the pundits, though one or two adventurous spirits, like R. E. M. Wheeler, welcomed it from the start; that by degrees ridicule and opposition died away; and that in 1930 the Congress of Archaeological Societies, through its Research Committee, drew up a report covering every department of archaeological field-work in Britain and offering archaeologists all over the country advice as to what the problems were, in each period, upon which the experts assembled in the committee thought it desirable to concentrate. The principle of question and answer had been officially adopted by British archaeology. Since then, the London Institute of Archaeology has come into existence; and I hope that if I told the students there how that principle was received, when I began to state it at Burlington House in the twenties, they would think me not only an old bore but an old liar into the bargain.

About the future of this principle among scholars

I am, accordingly, not anxious. When the scholars have got it firmly into their heads, the public will follow suit; and when they do, we may perhaps hope that they will in time compel the Government officials responsible for looking after our ancient monuments to treat them not as objects of sentimental pilgrimage but as potential sources of historical knowledge.

But we must not allow our hopes to run very high. We are no longer living in the nineteenth century, when public opinion could influence the activities of Government officials through the medium of Parliament. Every man who is engaged in scientific work of any kind knows that it is a fundamental obligation of scientific morality to publish your results. When the work is archaeological excavation the duty is a peculiarly urgent one, because a site once thoroughly excavated is a site from which no future archaeologist will ever be able to find out anything. All archaeologists know this, and all except the official archaeologists of the British Government act accordingly. But British Government archaeologists are constantly excavating sites all over the country, at the taxpayer's expense, without publishing any reports at all. They know that they are committing the fundamental crime against their own science; because when other archaeologists speak to them about it they have their excuse ready. The Treasury will not allow them money for publication.

A second principle was that, since history proper is the history of thought, there are no mere 'events' in history: what is miscalled an 'event' is really an action, and expresses some thought (intention, purpose) of its agent; the historian's business is therefore to identify this thought.[1]

For the archaeologist this means that all objects must be interpreted in terms of purposes. Whenever you find any object you must ask, 'What was it for?' and, arising out of that question, 'Was it good or bad for it? i.e. was the purpose embodied in it successfully embodied in it, or unsuccessfully?' These questions, being historical questions, must be answered not by guesswork but on historical evidence; any one who answers them must be able to show that his answer is the answer which the evidence demands.

This was the tritest of commonplaces. But the attempt to put it consistently into practice led to some interesting results. For example, the many archaeologists who had worked at the Roman Wall between Tyne and Solway had never, I found, seriously asked themselves what it was for. Vaguely, you could of course call it a frontier defence, and say that it was to keep out the tribes beyond it. But that will no more satisfy the historian than it will satisfy an engineer if you tell him that a marine engine is to drive a ship. How did it work? Was it meant to work, for example,

---

[1] Some 'events' of interest to the historian are not actions but the opposite, for which we have no English word: not *actiones* but *passiones*, instances of being acted upon. Thus the eruption of Vesuvius in A.D. 79 is to the historian a *passio* on the part of the people affected by it. It becomes an 'historical event' in so far as people were not merely affected by it, but reacted to this affection by actions of various kinds. The historian of the eruption is in reality the historian of these actions.

like a town-wall, from the top of which defenders repelled attacks? Several obvious features about it made it quite impossible that any Roman soldier should ever have meant to use it in that way. No one seemed to have noticed this before; but when I pointed it out in 1921[1] every one who was interested in the subject admitted that it was so, and my counter-suggestion that the wall was meant for an 'elevated sentry-walk' was generally accepted.

A question answered causes another question to arise. If the Wall was a sentry-walk, elevated from the ground and provided (no doubt) with a parapet to protect the sentries against sniping, the same sentry-walk must have continued down the Cumberland coast, beyond Bowness-on-Solway, in order to keep watch on vessels moving in the estuary; for it would have been very easy for raiders to sail across and land at any unguarded point between Bowness and St. Bee's Head. But here the sentry-walk need not be elevated, for sniping was not to be feared. There ought, therefore, to be a chain of towers, not connected by a wall but otherwise resembling those on the Wall, stretching down that coast. The question was, did such towers exist?

Search in old archaeological publications showed that towers of exactly the right kind had been found; but their existence had been forgotten, as generally happens with things whose purpose is not understood. Search on the ground in 1928 revealed a number of

[1] 'The Purpose of the Roman Wall', in *The Vasculum*, vol. viii, no. 1 (Newcastle-upon-Tyne), pp. 4–9.

other places where it seemed possible that others might yet be revealed by future excavation.[1]

Sometimes the attempt to work on this principle led me into trouble. I thought I could understand the strategical purpose of the Tyne–Solway Roman Wall easily enough. As completed by the chain of signal-stations on the Cumberland coast, it would have been very difficult to turn at either end; and if in addition to sentries on the look-out for enemy concentrations beyond it there were compact striking-forces in its attached forts, ready to march out and break them up, it would make a very efficient line of frontier defence. But when I asked my Scottish colleagues (or myself for that matter) the same question about the Forth–Clyde Wall, I got no answer. Sir George Macdonald, the acknowledged king of Scottish archaeologists, published the splendid second edition of his *Roman Wall in Scotland* in 1934; but my question is not asked there, nor even answered by implication. In the *Oxford History of England* I tried at least to state it and to point out some of the conditions for any possible solution. I even suggested a solution of my own. It was not well received by my friends over the Border. Whether they were right to reject it I do not know. But I do know that I was right to ask the question, and that it has got to be answered.

The principle applies not merely to archaeology, but to every kind of history. Where written sources are used, it implies that any action attributed by the

---

[1] 'Roman Signal-stations on the Cumberland Coast', in *Cumb. and West. Antiq. Soc. Trans.* xxix (1929), 138–65.

sources to any character must be understood in the same way. Julius Caesar, we are told, invaded Britain in two successive years. What did he do it for? The question is hardly ever asked by historians; and I can remember none who has tried to answer it scientifically, that is, by means of evidence. There is, of course, no evidence to speak of except that contained in Julius Caesar's own narrative. There he never says what he meant to effect by his invasions of Britain. It is the fact of his silence that constitutes our chief evidence as to what his intention was. Whatever he meant to bring about, his intention was one which he decided to conceal from his readers. In the light of a general acquaintance with the *Commentaries*, the likeliest explanation for this concealment was that whatever his purpose had been he had failed to achieve it. I then compared the strength of his expeditionary force with that of the army sent over by Claudius, nearly a century later, and this settled it. Caesar must have intended no mere punitive expedition or demonstration of force, like that of his German expedition in 55, but the complete conquest of the country. Once more, this view of mine may be mistaken; but future historians will have to reckon with the question I have raised, and either accept my answer or produce a better one.

People who do not understand historical thinking, but are obsessed by scissors and paste, will say: 'It is useless to raise the question, because if your only information comes from Caesar, and Caesar has not told you his plans, you cannot ever know what they were.' These are the people who, if they met you one Saturday afternoon with a fishing-rod, creel, and camp-stool, walking towards the river, would ask: 'Going fishing?' And I suppose that if they were serving on a jury when some one was tried for attempted murder because he had put arsenic in his wife's tea on Monday, and cyanide of potassium in her coffee on Tuesday, and on Wednesday broke her spectacles with a revolver-bullet, and knocked a piece out of her right ear with another on Thursday, and now pleaded not guilty, they would press for his acquittal because as he never admitted that he meant to murder her there could be no evidence that he did mean to.

A third principle was that no historical problem should be studied without studying what I called its second-order history; that is, the history of historical thought about it. This, too, was a pretty obvious re-mark. No undergraduate would write his tutor an essay on the battle of Marathon without first finding out what other people had said about it. If he did this preliminary work well, the result would be a history of research on Marathon. It would recount the differ-ent 'theories' that had been put forward, and would show how one of them had been abandoned owing to the 'difficulties' it entailed, and how another had arisen out of the attempt to remove those difficulties. By degrees second-order history, or the history of history, seemed more and more important to me; finally it took definitive shape as the conception into which I resolved that of 'historical criticism' in all its forms. Just as philosophical criticism resolved itself into the history of philosophy, so historical criticism resolved itself into the history of history.

In describing these researches into historical method, I am taking most of my examples from archaeology (that is, history in which the sources used are 'unwritten' sources, or, more accurately, are not pre-existing narratives of the events into which the historian is inquiring). But this is not because my results did not equally apply to history whose sources are 'written'. The reason I am talking so much about archaeology is that in archaeology the issue raised by the project of a Baconian revolution is unmistakable. When history is based on literary sources the difference between scissors-and-paste or pre-Baconian history, where the historian merely repeats what his 'authorities' tell him, and scientific or Baconian history, where he forces his 'authorities' to answer the questions he puts to them, is not always quite clear. It becomes clear enough on occasion; for example, when he tries to get out of his authorities' the answer to a question which they did not expect a reader to ask (as when we try to get out of an ancient writer answers to economic and demographic questions), or when he tries to get out of them facts which they wished to conceal. On other occasions it sometimes does not leap to the eye. In archaeology, however, it is obvious. Unless the archaeologist is content merely to describe what he or some one else has found, which it is almost impossible to do without using some interpretative terms implying purpose, like 'wall', 'pottery', 'implement', 'hearth', he is practising Baconian history all the time: asking about everything he handles, 'What was this for?' and trying to see how it fitted into the context of a peculiar kind of life.

For this reason archaeology has provided a wonderfully sensitive method for answering questions to which not only do literary sources give no direct answer, but which cannot be answered even by the most ingenious interpretation of them. The modern historian wants to ask all kinds of questions which are at bottom statistical questions. Was the population of a certain country at a certain time dense or rare? Was it increasing or diminishing? What did the people look like, or rather what different physical types were there among them, and which type predominated? What did they trade in, and with whom, and to what extent? Could they read and write, and how much? For Graeco-Roman antiquity, or even for the Middle Ages, no attempt to answer these questions on the basis of contemporary literary sources is of the smallest value. They are statistical questions, and the sources out of which you would be trying to answer them were written by men who were not statistically minded. For a writer under the Roman Empire the statement 'the population is diminishing' is not a statement about population statistics, it is a statement about some way in which he feels, like the statement so often made by writers of letters to the newspapers: 'We do not have such fine summers as we did when I was young.' Imagine a future meteorologist trying to compile an account of climatic changes from these letters, in the absence of meteorological statistics, and you will see the uselessness of the traditional demographic studies in ancient history.

If you want to answer statistical questions you must have statistical evidence. And that is something the archaeologist can provide when his work has attained a certain volume. In England, where Roman archaeology has gone forward incessantly in most parts of the country ever since the seventeenth century, there is a gigantic bulk of material from which many questions of this kind can be answered, if not conclusively, at least within a reasonable margin of error. In 1929, when thanks to the bold initiative and unwearying toil of O. G. S. Crawford—to whom future generations can never sufficiently realize their indebtedness —this material was plotted on the Ordnance Map of Roman Britain, it occurred to me[1] that it could be treated statistically and, when thus treated, used as a basis for an estimate of the total population of Roman Britain. I put it at half a million. There was a deluge of comment and criticism, partly in print, partly in letters. The only critics who gave me any reason to take them seriously urged that my figure was too low. I am now convinced that it was, and would advance it to a million. None of my critics demanded more than a million and a half. If the discrepancy between these figures appears large, let me remind the reader that three different historians, working from literary sources, have estimated the population of Roman Gaul at three million, six million, and thirty million respectively.

[1] 'Town and Country in Roman Britain', *Antiquity*, iii. 261–76.

In the same paper I tried to answer another statistical question, or group of questions, of a more complicated kind. What proportion of the inhabitants of Roman Britain were town-dwellers and country-dwellers respectively? And how did these proportions vary at different times during the period of Roman rule? This implied (1) a statistical survey of all the known Romano-British towns, directed to ascertaining their total population; and (2) an historical survey of the same, directed to ascertaining how that population increased or decreased at different times. Silchester was, and still is, the only such town whose entire surface has been covered by excavation, but it gave me no data for (2), and even its data for (1) were discounted by a certain difference of opinion as to whether the excavators had or had not found numerous dwellings not marked on any of their plans. My only reliable data were therefore derived from later diggings at Caerwent and Wroxeter. In both cases evidence had been found, though its full bearing had not been previously understood, that the development of the town had reached a peak early in its history, followed by a very long period of stagnation and progressive depopulation and decay. I argued that what was true of these towns might possibly prove true of the rest, and that in any case an economic historian would expect some such history, because the population implied by the size and character of these towns at their greatest extent was so disproportionate to the entire population of the country that their prosperity must have been unstable, and their origin due to a somewhat short-sighted policy of urbanization carried through in a doctrinaire spirit by the central government. Questions of this kind about Roman Britain had never been asked before, and some people apparently thought it would have been better if they had not been asked then. But subsequent excavation on Romano-British towns has justified my questions and on all essential points has confirmed my answers.

I will quote one other illustration of the way in which my principles of historical methodology led me to an entirely new treatment of archaeological material.

Haverfield had shown, as everybody now knew, that there had been a 'Romanization' of Britain: that a civilization of Celtic type had been replaced by one of the 'cosmopolitan' pattern to be found, with local differences but not very important ones, in any province of the Roman Empire. In the matter of arts and crafts, for example, Celtic fashions had been followed with a high degree of artistic talent before the Roman conquest. After the conquest, these were shortly replaced by Roman provincial fashions. There was also, Haverfield pointed out, a 'Celtic Revival' towards the end of the period and after it. This, too, was by now a matter of common knowledge.

This was puzzling. If a kind of cultural steam-roller had flattened the Celtic taste out of the Britons, and they had learnt to adopt the taste of the Roman Empire, why should they go Celtic again three centuries later? And indeed how could they? When once a tradition has died, how can it come to life again, except through the rise of archaizing fashions, which in this case we may safely rule out? If by (say) 1920 English peasants had stopped singing modal folk-songs, and had taken instead to hearing dance-music on the wireless; and if no one had written their songs down and preserved them in libraries; would it not be very odd to find their descendants beginning to sing modal folk-songs again round about the year 2200?

In 1935, when I was writing my part of the *Oxford History of England*, the problem had lately become a fashionable one, and many first-class archaeologists had tried to solve it. Their attempts fell into three classes.

First, there were those who regarded the case as a perfectly normal one of survival. The tradition of Celtic design, they suggested, had never been broken. True, we lacked evidence for this. There were, indeed, objects dating between A.D. 150 and 300 which bore patterns in the Celtic manner, but they were very few and could not be taken to prove the continued existence of a school of Celtic decoration. But all these were of metal. Celtic designs might very well have survived in common use among textile-workers and wood-carvers, and been reintroduced from them into the trades whose products have come into our hands and made us talk of a Celtic revival.

This attempt was sound, in so far as it was based on the sound principle that revival implies survival. But it ended in failure, because the evidence of survival was not forthcoming, and no historian is entitled to draw cheques in his own favour on evidence that he does not possess, however lively his hopes that it may hereafter be discovered. He must argue from the evidence he has, or stop arguing.

Secondly, there were those who pointed out that not all the Celts were subjected to the Roman steam-roller. Why should not the traditions of Celtic art have survived in unconquered Caledonia, and thence have re-entered Roman Britain with Pictish invaders when the frontier defence broke down? Once more, a very reasonable suggestion, but for the lack of evidence. The districts in which we have evidence for a Celtic revival are those farthest away from the frontier, and Pictland offers no models or originals out of which that revival might have grown.

Thirdly, there were those who argued that Celtic art was a product of the 'Celtic temperament', and that the Celtic temperament blossomed into artistic expression only under conditions of a certain kind. These conditions had existed at the beginning of the Roman period and again at its end; but not in between. It only remained to say what the conditions were. This argument I valued for its intriguing suggestion that the survival of a certain style in art does not necessarily depend on the survival of certain patterns in workshop practice; but its dependence on an occult entity like the 'Celtic temperament' forbade me to take it seriously. With entities of that kind we have left behind us the daylight, and even the twilight, of history, and have entered a darkness peopled by all the monsters of *Rassentheorie* and Jungian psychology. In that darkness what we find is not history but the negation of history; not the solution of historical problems, but only a heady drink which gives us the illusion of having solved them.

The unsolved problem, focusing as it did the whole problem of Romanization (what exactly does Romanization mean? What was it that really happened to people when they became what is called Romanized?) focused also for me the whole problem of art-history and indeed of what the Germans call history of culture. There seemed to be no hope of solving it unless you had first of all settled certain questions of principle. And when I turned my thoughts towards the planning of my chapter on 'Art' in the Oxford History, I deliberately set aside the particular problem until I had cleared up my mind about the principles involved.

If you want to know why a certain kind of thing happened in a certain kind of case, you must begin by asking, 'What did you expect?' You must consider what the normal development is in cases of that kind. Only then, if the thing that happened in this case was exceptional, should you try to explain it by appeal to exceptional conditions.

Now, it seemed to me possible that the difficulty in this case was an illusory difficulty, due to the fact that the nature of historical process was misconceived. As I had long ago proved in the *Libellus de Generatione*, any process involving an historical change from P_1 to P_2 leaves an unconverted residue of P_1 incapsu-

lated within an historical state of things which super-
ficially is altogether P_2. This, I thought, might prove
the key to my problem.

Incapsulation is not an 'occult entity'. It was my
name for such facts as this—familiar enough to everybody—that a man who changes his habits, thoughts,
&c., retains in the second phase some residue of the
first. He gives up smoking, but his desire to smoke
does not thereupon disappear. In his subsequent life
the desire is what I call incapsulated. It survives, and
it produces results; but these results are not what
they were before he gave up smoking. They do not
consist in smoking. The desire survives in the form
of an unsatisfied desire. If, after a time, he is again
found to be smoking, that need not prove that he never
left off; it may very well be because he never lost the
desire, and when the reasons against satisfying the
desire disappeared he began once more to satisfy it.

Without any implications as to racial temperament
or a 'racial unconscious' the same kind of thing may
happen in a society. If the members of a certain
society have been in the habit of acting or thinking in
certain ways, and if at a certain time they try to stop
acting and thinking in those ways, and do their best
to act and think in different ways, the desire to go on
acting and thinking in the old way will probably persist. It will certainly persist, and persist in a lively
form, if they were accustomed to think and act in those
ways very effectively and found great satisfaction in
doing so. The tendency to revert to the old ways
would in that case be strong.

Now you might think that, unless some occult entity like a racial temperament or an inheritance of acquired psychical characteristics were at work, this tendency would not survive into the second generation. You might think that, even though the original converts never entirely got rid of the old Adam, their children would start fair. You might think that although the fathers had eaten a good many wild oats in their time, the children's teeth would not be set on edge. They would imbibe the new ways of thinking and acting with their mothers' milk, and feel no temptation to think or act otherwise.

Well, you would be wrong. Suppose a very war-like people, at a certain crisis in its history, turned completely peaceful. In the first generation, warlike impulses would survive; but let us suppose them sternly repressed, so that everybody behaved in an entirely peaceful manner. When the people of this generation set to work on the moral education of their children, the children would be carefully told that they must on no account indulge in the forbidden pleasures of war. 'But what is war, Daddy?' Then Daddy gives a description of war, emphasizing its wrongness, but (doubtless altogether against his will) making it very plain to his innocent offspring that war was a grand thing while it lasted and that he would love to fight his neighbours again if only he did not know that he ought not. The children are quick to understand all that. They not only learn what war is, or was, but they learn also that it is, or was, a grand thing, though of course wrong; and they carefully pass all this on to their own children when the time comes. Thus the transmission by educational means of any moral ideal which involves the outlawry of an institution or custom, and the repression of a desire for it, entails the simultaneous transmission of that desire itself. The children of each generation are taught to want what they are taught they must not have.

In time, the tradition which keeps alive the memory of the forbidden thing, and keeps alive at the same time the desire for it, may die out. Its disappearance will be greatly accelerated if the new way of thinking and acting proves to be one in which the converts find themselves successful and satisfied. In that case the 'folk-memory' (nothing occult; nothing inborn; simply the transmission by example and precept of certain ways of thinking and acting from generation to generation) of a success and satisfaction now no longer permitted will tend to fade away. Where you find the new ways of thinking and acting never displayed with more than a low degree of success, you may take it as certain that the discarded ways are remembered with regret, and that the tradition of their glories is being tenaciously kept alive.

So much for generalities. There are some who will say, 'You are talking psychology, and you ought to ask a psychologist whether what you are saying is true or not.' But I am not talking psychology, and shall not ask help from its exponents; for I regard the kind of psychology that deals with this kind of question as a sham science. I am talking history.

Applying this to the case in point, I found it possible to assert a connexion between two facts, both of them notorious, which had not previously been thought of as connected. One was the Celtic revival; the other was the badness of Romanizing British art. The badness of Romanizing British art, as I say, was notorious; but my own study of it had the unforeseen effèct of removing from it the only really valuable asset with which it had been credited. Its recognized masterpiece was the famous Bath Gorgon, which scholars had tried, quite in vain, to connect with prototypes in 'classical' art. I was able to prove that the inspiration of this fine work was not 'classical' but Celtic; and at the same time I suggested that it was probably the work not of a British sculptor but of a Gaul.

The general position I have already laid down implies that the less successful the Britons were in Romanizing art, granted always their very conspicuous earlier success in art of the Celtic type, and granted also the sharp opposition between the symbolic and no doubt magical character of Celtic design and the naturalistic and merely amusing character of the 'Woolworth art' of the Roman empire, the more they were likely to cherish the memory of their own fashions and ensure that these fashions were never wholly lost to sight by the rising generation.

This was the idea which I expressed in the chapter on 'Art' in the *Oxford History of England*; a chapter which I would gladly leave as the sole memorial of my Romano-British studies, and the best example I can give to posterity of how to solve a much-debated problem in history, not by discovering fresh evidence, but by reconsidering questions of principle. It may thus serve to illustrate what I have called the *rapprochement* between philosophy and history, as seen from the point of view of history.

These books summed up the results of innumerable studies, many of which were reported in greater detail in about a hundred articles and pamphlets mostly written between 1920 and 1930. But the main bulk of my work on Roman Britain went into the Corpus of Inscriptions. Haverfield, almost immediately before his death, had decided to publish a new collection of all the Roman inscriptions (excluding those brought from abroad in modern times) in Britain; and thinking it desirable that each should be illustrated with a facsimile drawing—for he had no illusions about the value of photographic illustrations in a work of this kind—he asked me to serve as draughtsman. After his death I decided to go on with the work, and from 1920 onwards I spent much time every year travelling about the country and drawing Roman inscriptions.

The detailed knowledge of the subject which I acquired, and the practice in deciphering inscriptions, many of them extremely difficult to read, were invaluable to me. But the inscriptions themselves were not of very great service to my Romano-British studies. The use of epigraphic material is a magnificent exercise for an historian just beginning to shake himself free from the scissors-and-paste mentality, which is why it developed in so wonderful a manner in the late nineteenth century; but the epigraphic historian as such can never be wholly Baconian in spirit. Regarded as documents, inscriptions tell you less, under critical scrutiny, than literary texts; regarded as relics, they tell you less than archaeological material proper. And on the questions which I particularly wanted to ask, it happened that inscriptions threw hardly any light. I felt, therefore, that by my work on Romano-British inscriptions I was rather building a monument to the past, to the great spirits of Mommsen and Haverfield, than forging a weapon for the future.

XII

THEORY AND PRACTICE

In addition to the *rapprochement* between philosophy and history, whose earlier stages I have already tried to describe, I was also working at a *rapprochement* between theory and practice. My first efforts in this direction were attempts to obey what I felt as a call to resist the moral corruption propagated by the 'realist' dogma that moral philosophy does no more than study in a purely theoretical spirit a subject-matter which it leaves wholly unaffected by that investigation.

The opposite of this dogma seemed to me not only a truth, but a truth which, for the sake of his integrity and efficacy as a moral agent in the wider sense of that term, ought to be familiar to every human being: namely, that in his capacity as a moral, political, or economic agent he lives not in a world of 'hard facts' to which 'thoughts' make no difference, but in a world of 'thoughts'; that if you change the moral, political, and economic 'theories' generally accepted by the society in which he lives, you change the character of his world; and that if you change his own 'theories' you change his relation to that world; so that in either case you change the ways in which he acts.

The 'realist' attempt to deny this could, no doubt, be defended with some plausibility, so long as a clean cut could be made between philosophical and historical thinking. It could be admitted that the way in which a man acts, in so far as he is a moral, political, economic agent, is not independent of the way in which he thinks of the situation in which he finds himself. If knowledge as to the facts of one's situation is called historical knowledge, historical knowledge is necessary to action. But it could still be argued that philosophical thinking, which has to do with timeless 'universals', is not necessary.

Arguments of this kind were no longer even worth refuting, once I knew that 'realism' was completely astray as to the nature of history, and that consequently any 'realist' argument based on the distinction between history and philosophy, or 'facts' and 'theories', or 'the individual' (which some 'realists' miscalled 'the particular') and 'the universal', must be regarded as suspect. Immediately after the War, therefore, I began to reconsider in detail all the familiar topics and problems of moral philosophy, including under that head the theory of economics and that of politics, as well as that of morals in the narrower sense, on the principles which by now were controlling all my work.

In the first place, I subjected these topics and problems to what I called an historical treatment, insisting that every one of them had its history and was unintelligible without some knowledge of that history. Secondly, I attempted to treat them in another way, which I called analytic. My notion was that one and the same action, which as action pure and simple was a 'moral' action, was also a 'political' action as action relative to a rule, and at the same time an

'economic' action as means to an end. The problems
of moral theory, in the broader sense of the word
moral, could thus be divided into (*a*) problems of
moral theory in the narrower sense, that is, problems
concerned with action as such; (*b*) problems of political theory, that is, problems concerned with action
as the making, obeying, or breaking of rules; and
(*c*) problems of economic theory, or problems concerned with action as the procuring or non-procuring
of ends beyond itself.

There were, I held, no merely moral actions, no
merely political actions, and no merely economic
actions. Every action was moral, political, and economic. But although actions were not to be divided
into three separate classes—the moral, the political,
and the economic—these three characteristics, their
morality, their politicality, and their economicity,
must be distinguished and not confused as they are,
for example, by utilitarianism, which offers an account of economicity when professing to offer one of
morality.

These were the lines on which I treated the subject
in my lectures of 1919. I continued to lecture upon
it yearly during almost the whole remainder of my
life at Pembroke College, with constant revision. The
scheme I have just described obviously represents
a stage in my thought at which the *rapprochement*
between history and philosophy was very incomplete.
Any reader who has understood the earlier chapters
of this book can see for himself how I modified it as
time went on.

The *rapprochement* between theory and practice was equally incomplete. I no longer thought of them as mutually independent: I saw that the relation between them was one of intimate and mutual dependence, thought depending upon what the thinker learned by experience in action, action depending upon how he thought of himself and the world; I knew very well, too, that scientific, historical, or philosophical thinking depended quite as much on 'moral' qualities as on 'intellectual' ones, and that 'moral' difficulties were to be overcome not by 'moral' force alone but by clear thinking.

But this was only a theoretical *rapprochement* of theory and practice, not a practical one. I still conducted my daily life as if I thought that the business of that life was theoretical and not practical. I did not see that my attempted reconstruction of moral philosophy would remain incomplete so long as my habits were based on the vulgar division of men into thinkers and men of action.

This division, like so much that nowadays we take for granted, was a survival from the Middle Ages. I lived and worked in a University; and a University is an institution based on medieval ideas, whose life and work are still hedged about by the medieval interpretation of the Greek distinction between the contemplative life and the practical life as a division between two classes of specialists.

I can now see that I had three different attitudes towards this survival. There was a first R. G. C. who knew in his philosophy that the division was false, and that 'theory' and 'practice', being mutually dependent, must both alike suffer frustration if segregated into the specialized functions of different classes.

There was a second R. G. C. who in the habits of his daily life behaved as if it had been sound; living as a professional thinker whose college gate symbolized his aloofness from the affairs of practical life. My philosophy and my habits were thus in conflict; I lived as if I disbelieved my own philosophy, and philosophized as if I had not been the professional thinker that in fact I was. My wife used to tell me so; and I used to be a good deal annoyed.

But underneath this conflict there was a third R. G. C., for whom the gown of the professional thinker was a disguise alternately comical and disgusting in its inappropriateness. This third R. G. C. was a man of action, or rather he was something in which the difference between thinker and man of action disappeared. He never left me alone for very long. He turned over in his sleep, and the fabric of my habitual life began to crack. He dreamed, and his dreams crystallized into my philosophy. When he would not lie quiet and let me play at being a don, I would appease him by throwing off my academic associations and going back to my own part of the country to address the local antiquarian society. It may seem an odd form of 'release' for a suppressed man of action; but it was a very effective one. The enthusiasm for historical studies, and for myself as their leader in those studies, which I never failed to arouse in my audiences, was not in principle different from the enthusiasm for his person and his policy which is aroused by a successful political speaker. And sometimes this third R. G. C. woke right up; for example, on a day soon after the beginning of August 1914, when a crowd of Northumberland coal-miners, full of patriotic fervour, saw what they imagined to be a German spy on 'the old Roman camp' up the hill, and took appropriate action.

The third R. G. C. used to stand up and cheer, in a sleepy voice, whenever I began reading Marx. I was never at all convinced either by Marx's metaphysics or by his economics; but the man was a fighter, and a grand one; and no mere fighter, but a fighting philosopher. His philosophy might be unconvincing; but to whom was it unconvincing? Any philosophy, I knew, would be not only unconvincing but nonsensical to a person who misunderstood the problem it was meant to solve. Marx's was meant to solve a 'practical' problem; its business, as he said himself, was to 'make the world better'. Marx's philosophy would necessarily, therefore, appear nonsensical except to a person who, I will not say shared his desire to make the world better by means of a philosophy, but at least regarded that desire as a reasonable one. According to my own principles of philosophical criticism, it was inevitable that Marx's philosophy should appear nonsensical to gloves-on philosophers like the 'realists', with their sharp division between theory and practice, or the 'liberals', such as John Stuart Mill, who argued that people ought to be allowed to think whatever they liked because it didn't really matter what they thought. In order to criticize a gloves-off philosophy like that of Marx, you must be at least enough of a gloves-off philosopher to think gloves-off philosophizing legitimate.

The first and third R. G. C.s agreed in wanting a gloves-off philosophy. They did not want a philosophy that should be a scientific toy guaranteed to amuse professional thinkers safe behind their college gates. They wanted a philosophy that should be a weapon. So far, I was with Marx. Perhaps all that stood in the way of a closer agreement was the second R. G. C., the academic or professional thinker.

My attitude towards politics had always been what in England is called democratic and on the Continent liberal. I regarded myself as a unit in a political system where every citizen possessing the franchise had the duty of voting for a representative to parliament. I thought that the government of my country, owing to a wide franchise, a free press, and a universally recognized right of free speech, was such as to make it impossible that any considerable section should be oppressed by government action, or that their grievances should be hushed up, even if a remedy for them could not be found. I thought that the democratic system was not only a form of government but a school of political experience coextensive with the nation, and I thought that no authoritarian government, however strong, could be so strong as one which rested on a politically educated public opinion. As a form of government, I thought its essence lay in the fact that it was a nursery-garden where policies were brought to maturity in the open air, not a post office for distributing ready-made policies to a passively receptive country.

These I thought very great merits; greater than those of any other political system yet devised, and worth defending at all costs against people who, because they wished to hoodwink the citizen and enforce upon him ready-made policies devised by some irresponsible cabal, untruthfully accused it of being 'cumbrous' and 'inefficient'. I knew, of course, that Marx had denounced it as a fraud, whose business was to throw a semblance of legality over the oppression of the workers by the capitalists; but although I knew that such oppression existed and was to a great extent legalized, I thought that the business of a democratic government was to eradicate it.

I did not think that our constitution was free from faults. But the discovery and correction of these faults was the function of governments, not of individual voters. For the system was a self-correcting one, charged with amending its own faults by legislation. It was also a self-feeding one. Members of parliament were chosen by the voters from among themselves; higher grades in the system were filled from among the members of parliament; and thus, so long as the individual voters did their political duty by keeping themselves adequately informed on public questions, and voting in accordance with their judgement as to where on any given occasion the good of the nation as a whole was to be sought, there was little danger that their representatives would be insufficiently informed, or insufficiently endowed with public spirit, to do their work creditably. And owing to the majority vote it did not matter if a few, at any stage, were ignorant or misguided. So long as the majority were well enough informed and public-spirited enough for what they had to do, fools and knaves would be outvoted.

The whole system, however, would break down if a majority of the electorate should become either ill informed on public questions or corrupt in their attitude towards them: by which I mean, capable of adopting towards them a policy directed not to the good of the nation as a whole, but to the good of their own class or section or of themselves.

In the first respect, I became conscious of a change for the worse during the eighteen-nineties. The newspapers of the Victorian age made it their first business to give their readers full and accurate information about matters of public concern. Then came the *Daily Mail*, the first English newspaper for which the word 'news' lost its old meaning of facts which a reader ought to know if he was to vote intelligently, and acquired the new meaning of facts, or fictions, which it might amuse him to read. By reading such a paper, he was no longer teaching himself to vote. He was teaching himself not to vote; for he was teaching himself to think of 'the news' not as the situation in which he was to act, but as a mere spectacle for idle moments.

In the second respect, I became aware of corrupting influences rather later. The South African settlement of the Campbell-Bannerman ministry was a fine exhibition of the principles in which I believed, and a proof that I was not wrong in thinking them to be the principles of English policy. The social legislation of its successor, Asquith's first ministry, was such as I could not but approve. But the way in which it was advertised, by promising voters 'ninepence for fourpence', was the negation of those principles. Mr. Lloyd George became to me a landmark, second only to the *Daily Mail*, in the corruption of the electorate. During the first quarter of the present century, each of these corrupting influences underwent enormous development.

After the War the democratic system was threatened by two powerful rivals. There were two elements in that system, one of which was inherited by each rival. On a Lockian basis of private property the democratic tradition had erected a system of representative institutions designed to promote the good of the nation as a whole. But there existed, on paper since Marx formulated it, and in terms of political fact since the Russian revolution, a system having the same end but a different starting-point. The Socialists (I use the term as implying Marxian Socialism) agreed with the democratic tradition in aiming at social and economic betterment for the entire people, but proposed to achieve this aim through the public ownership of 'means of production'. Then came Fascism in Italy and National Socialism in Germany, which agreed with the democratic tradition in making private property their first principle; but in order to preserve it they abandoned, not only the political institutions of democratic government, but also the aim of social and economic betterment upon which those institutions had been directed.

The real breach between the democratic tradition and the Socialists was not on a point of policy but on a point of fact. No one, I think, would deny that modern European society is divided into people whose energies are focused on owning things, and people whose energies are focused on doing things. Let these be called capitalists and workers respectively. All capitalists do things, and all workers own things; but this does not obliterate the distinction. If what is vital to a man is his ownership of certain things, while his engaging in certain activities is relatively unimportant, he is a capitalist, however much he does. If the contrary, he is a worker, however much he owns.

Between these two 'classes' in modern European society, the Socialists held that there was in existence a 'class war', and that parliamentary institutions only disguised this war and did not overcome it. The democratic tradition maintained that parliamentary institutions acted in such a way as to dissipate any tendency to class war by means of free speech and open discussion. Fascism on this point agreed with Socialism; though its mouthpieces, pursuing their declared policy of deceit, denied it. But whereas Socialism hoped to end the class war by a workers' victory leading to the abolition of class distinctions, Fascism hoped to perpetuate it by a capitalist victory leading to the permanent subjection of the workers. National Socialism is only the local German variety of Fascism.

Fascism could best be understood as a capitalist Socialism: a system in which the machinery of Socialism had been turned upside down in order to connect it up with a different prime mover, namely, the desire of capitalists to remain capitalists. In order to gratify this desire they were glad to pay blackmail to the Fascist state far in excess of any taxation and control ever devised by parliamentary government. In Socialism, the prime mover was the desire for the whole nation's social and economic welfare. By comparison with this, the motive power of Fascism was not respectable, and had to be disguised. It was therefore concealed beneath a cloak of international hatred and jealousy.

Actually, Fascism was not compatible with international hatred. It was based not on the idea of nation but on the idea of class; and had it been honest, it would have answered the Communists' Manifesto with the call, 'Capitalists of the world, unite.'

But Fascism was not capable of honesty. Essentially an attempt to fight Socialism with its own weapons, it was always inconsistent with itself. There was once a very able and distinguished philosopher who was converted to Fascism. As a philosopher, that was the end of him. No one could embrace a creed so fundamentally muddle-headed and remain capable of clear thinking. The great exponents of

Fascism have been specialists in arousing mass-emotion; its minor adherents, tacticians and plotters.

Knowing all this, and thinking that in spite of some corrupting influences the true democratic tradition still existed in my own country, I rejected Socialism on the ground that the parliamentary system was still working well enough to perform its proper function of an antiseptic against class war; rejected Fascism as an incoherent caricature of Socialism's worst features; and stood by the democratic tradition.

'It was the Spanish ulcer', said Napoleon, 'that destroyed me.' I had travelled over large parts of Spain in 1930 and 1931, and in the latter year had seen revolutionary movements everywhere going on. They were being conducted in the most orderly fashion. My friends and I never saw or heard of a single act of violence, or a single piece of evidence that such acts had been done. In one town we watched what we took for a religious festival, at which children in white were singing while their elders looked on, respectfully interested and perfectly quiet. Later, in a wine-shop, with the wireless relaying evensong from Canterbury cathedral, we asked our fellow drinkers what the festival was. 'Festival?' said they. 'That was the Revolution.'

Our friends used to write from England expressing fears for our safety among the atrocities by which, the newspapers told them, the revolution was being accompanied; at the mercy of the bloodthirsty Communists in their war against religion. But there were no atrocities; no Communists to be seen or heard of, only democratically minded men at work establishing a parliamentary government; no war against religion, only a clean sweep of the old political domination by ecclesiastical and military bosses, while the Church itself, as one saw in every town, carried on its religious functions undisturbed, its buildings and its personnel in no way interfered with.

At the time, I thought it no more than comical that the English newspapers should be so ill informed about what was going on in Spain. It did not occur to me that another explanation was possible. I do not know which is the right one. Either it was a mere coincidence that this epidemic of journalistic ignorance prepared the way for the policy by which, later on, the larger part of the British press (acting, one cannot but suspect, under government instructions) deliberately deceived its readers as to the character of the Spanish republic; or else that policy was already working, and those instructions presumably issued, by 1931.

A few years later, the Spanish civil war began. It was a rebellion of the deposed military bosses against the democratic régime that had supplanted them: the rebellion of a nation's army against that nation's people and their properly constituted government; properly constituted, that is to say, according to English ideas. Every Englishman who had any faith in the English political tradition would, if he knew the truth, wish to help the Spanish government against the rebels. And very little help was needed; only a fair field. If

the government could once extemporize and equip
an army, the rebels' fate was sealed.

The British 'National' government prevented this
from happening. It adopted, and enforced on certain
other nations, a policy of 'non-intervention', which
meant forbidding the introduction into Spain of men
to fight and munitions to fight with. Now, if in a
certain country the army is in rebellion against an
unarmed government, which is trying to arm in its
own defence, no great penetration is needed in order
to see that an embargo against the importation of
arms into that country is an act of assistance to the
rebels. People in England saw that their government,
under its 'non-intervention' mask, was intervening,
and very energetically, on the rebels' side; so to keep
them quiet a press campaign began, repeating the
stories about Communism and atrocities for whose
falsity a few years earlier I could vouch. It was successful. People who believe in the English political
tradition do not like Communists and do not approve
of atrocities. Sympathy for the Spanish government
wilted visibly. No doubt, people said, it was only
our 'non-intervention' humbug that was enabling the
rebels to make headway against the government; but
did one really want the government to win?

Everybody knew that the rebel leader was a tool of
the Italian and German dictators; and that these,
whatever lip-service they gave to 'non-intervention',
were feeding him constantly with men and munitions.
Everybody knew that in doing so they had altered the
strategic situation in the Mediterranean, from the

British point of view, very greatly for the worse. But if anybody hinted at these things, the British 'National' government answered, 'Trust us; we know what we are doing; we have given you peace.' This, once more, was successful. The electorate was willing to put up with almost anything so long as war was averted. But no evidence was produced, either then or later, that it had been. No evidence was produced that either or both of the dictators bullied the British government into adopting the 'non-intervention' policy by threats of war. No evidence was produced that their own notorious refusal to abide by that policy was covered by threats of the same kind. No evidence was produced that the British government would have endangered peace by simply refraining from those actions by which, legally or illegally, it forbade its nationals to enlist in the Spanish government's service.

No evidence of these things was produced; and they were things which, certainly, no one would have believed at the time, and no one ever will believe, without evidence, and conclusive evidence, adduced to prove them. But so dense was the atmosphere of concealment in which the 'National' government had wrapped its policy for many years (beginning with the empty rodomontades of Ramsay MacDonald, who seemed to say so much and never said anything at all; and going on with the 'con-man' methods of Mr. Baldwin, who seldom said anything except what an honest man he was and how completely every one could trust him) that no one expected the government spokesmen even to say these things, let alone produce evidence for them. Nothing was definitely said, but a great deal was hinted.

But though nothing was said, much was done. Failing any statement of the 'National' government's policy, I found myself obliged to infer their policy from the evidence of their actions. This was not difficult. For any one accustomed to interpret evidence, their actions admitted only one explanation. They wanted the rebels to win, and wanted to conceal this fact from the electorate. They knew that the rebels could not win without help from themselves, so they gave that help. They knew that the rebels could not win without grave damage to British interests, so they sacrificed those interests.

Why were they so anxious for the rebels' success? Not because of 'the Communist menace', for although my old friend the *Daily Mail*, a keen supporter of the 'National' government, and now as ever a keen worker in the cause of corrupting the public mind, habitually referred to the Spanish government as 'Red', that is, Communist, the government knew as well as the *Daily Mail* did that republican Spain was not a Communist state but a parliamentary democracy, and that Señor Negrin's cabinet, for example, contained only one solitary communist, who was included after his party had joined in the general declaration of loyalty to democratic principles. The Spanish civil war was a straight fight between Fascist dictatorship and parliamentary democracy. The British government, behind all its disguises, had declared itself a partisan of Fascist dictatorship.

At the beginning of 1938, when this became clear to me, I formed no opinion as to how far individual members of that government knew what they were doing. Fascism, I repeat, is a muddle-headed business. I found it easy to believe that the 'National' government's policy of truckling to the Fascist powers, and of refusing to tell the country what they were doing, need not have arisen from that government's clear comprehension of its own aims, coupled with a clear understanding of their detestableness in the eyes of the country, and resulting in a clear decision that the country must be deceived. It might arise from imbecility of will and weakness of intellect, combined with certain sneaking admirations and certain unexamined timidities, a defective sense of responsibility, and a feeble and sometimes inoperative regard for the truth. If any one in 1937, or even early in 1938, had said to the prime minister, with a reminiscence of Dr. Johnson's repartee to the Thames waterman, 'Sir, your government, under pretence of inability to defend the national interests, is conducting a Fascist revolution', I dare say the prime minister would have denied the charge with all the sincerity that he possesses.

The events of 1938 taught me nothing about the 'National' government that I did not know already. I began the year in the expectation of two developments: an open clash between the prime minister and the principles of parliamentary government, and a more flagrant repetition, somewhere else, of the Spanish formula: aggression by a Fascist state, rendered successful by support from the British government under cover of a war-scare engineered by that government itself among the British people.

The first expectation was realized in the early summer, when in open defiance of the rules of parliamentary privilege a concerted attempt was made by members of the cabinet to suppress parliamentary criticism of the government's already notorious inefficiency in carrying out the rearmament programme, by threats of prosecution under the Official Secrets Act against Mr. Duncan Sandys, the member of parliament who had dared to criticize. The matter was discreetly hushed up in the government newspapers; but every one who had access to the facts knew that it meant war between a Fascist cabinet and the parliamentary constitution of the country it was ruling.

The second expectation was realized during the Czechoslovakia crisis in September, when the British prime minister flew successively to Berchtesgaden, Godesberg, and Munich, returning every time with orders in his pocket from the German dictator in obedience to which he changed the country's policy behind the back of parliament, and even of the cabinet.

To me, therefore, the betrayal of Czechoslovakia was only a third case of the same policy by which the 'National' government had betrayed Abyssinia and Spain; and I was less interested in the fact itself than in the methods by which it was accomplished: the carefully engineered war-scare in the country at large, officially launched by the simultaneous issue of gas-masks and of the prime minister's emotional broadcast, two days before his flight to Munich, and the carefully staged hysterical scene in parliament on the following night. These things were in the established tradition of Fascist dictatorial methods; except that whereas the Italian and German dictators sway mobs by appeal to the thirst for glory and national aggrandizement, the English prime minister did it by playing on sheer, stark terror.

He gained his point. At the time of writing, England has not formally bidden farewell to its parliamentary institutions; it has only permitted them to become inoperative. It has not renounced its faith in political liberty; it has only thrown away the thing in which it still professes to believe. It has not given away its Empire; it has only handed over the control of that Empire's communications to a jealous and grasping power. It has not ceased to have a voice in European affairs; it has only used that voice to further the ends of another power even more jealous and even more grasping.

This has been done not by the wish of the country, or of any considerable section in the country, but because the country has been tricked. To recall what I said on pp. 48–9, the forces which have been at work for nearly half a century corrupting the public mind, producing in it by degrees a willingness to forgo that full, prompt, and accurate information on matters of public importance which is the indispensable nourishment of a democratic society, and a disinclination to make decisions on such matters in the public-spirited frame of mind which is a democratic society's life-blood, have 'trained up a generation of Englishmen and Englishwomen' to be the dupes of a politician who has so successfully 'appealed to their emotions' by 'promises of private gain' (the gain of personal safety from the horrors of war) that they have allowed him to sacrifice their country's interests, throw away its prestige, and blacken its name in the face of the world, in order that he should glare out from his photographs with the well-known hypnotic eyes of a dictator.

It is not the business of this autobiography to ask how completely the country has in fact been deceived, or how long the present degree of deception will last. I am not writing an account of recent political events in England: I am writing a description of the way in which those events impinged upon myself and broke up my pose of a detached professional thinker. I know now that the minute philosophers of my youth, for all their profession of a purely scientific detachment from practical affairs, were the propagandists of a coming Fascism. I know that Fascism means the end of clear thinking and the triumph of irrationalism. I know that all my life I have been engaged unawares in a political struggle, fighting against these things in the dark. Henceforth I shall fight in the daylight.

INDEX